THE LEADER, THE TEACHER & YOU

Leadership Through the Third Generation

THE
LEADER,
THE
TEACHER
&
YOU

*Leadership Through the
Third Generation*

Siong Guan Lim

Lee Kuan Yew School of Public Policy,
National University of Singapore, Singapore

Joanne H. Lim

The Right Perspective, Singapore

 World Scientific

 Imperial College Press

Published by

Imperial College Press
57 Shelton Street
Covent Garden
London WC2H 9HE

Distributed by

World Scientific Publishing Co. Pte. Ltd.
5 Toh Tuck Link, Singapore 596224
USA office: 27 Warren Street, Suite 401-402, Hackensack, NJ 07601
UK office: 57 Shelton Street, Covent Garden, London WC2H 9HE

Library of Congress Control Number: 2013955832

British Library Cataloguing-in-Publication Data
A catalogue record for this book is available from the British Library.

THE LEADER, THE TEACHER & YOU
Leadership Through The Third Generation

ISBN 9781783263974
ISBN 9781783263776 (pbk)

Printed in Singapore

AFFIRMATIONS

AFFIRMATIONS

WHAT OTHER LEADERS ARE SAYING ABOUT THIS BOOK

"Everyone — regardless of profession — will benefit from reading this uniquely designed and highly original book. It is full of human insights, and it has a deep understanding of successful leadership, an appreciation of selflessness as the key to our collective future, an awareness of history's relevance to our lives and an unflinching emphasis on excellence. Siong Guan Lim is one of the most outstanding public servants in any country, and after finishing this book, you will know why."

Senator Bill Bradley
Former U.S. Senator and a Managing Director at Allen & Co.
United States of America

"The Leader, the Teacher and You is a riveting and thoughtful study on leadership based on theory, principles, and experience by a former Head of the Civil Service and one of Singapore's most successful and admired public servants, Siong Guan Lim. It should be read by every student of politics and public policy, and anyone who aspires to play a leadership role.

The book which as the author says is "part biography, part commentary, and part exposition," is loaded with insights into how to work with people, deal with reality, motivate an organisation, achieve results, anticipate change, and ensure relevance of the organisation.

For those who have long puzzled over how Singapore has been able to achieve so much with so little and in short time, it is public servants such as Siong Guan Lim who have made the partnership between the civil service and the elected politicians so fruitful.

Through his fascinating account of how he started in his first job as an engineer in the Sewerage Department, went on to be the Principal Private Secretary to Prime Minister Lee Kuan Yew, worked with Deputy Prime Minister and Minister of Defence Dr Goh Keng Swee, and became successively Permanent Secretary of Defence, Education, and Finance, he recounts the crucial mentorship and inspiration provided by Singapore's leaders. He thoroughly examines what true leadership is all about. Lim moved on to become Chairman of Singapore's Economic Development Board and then Group President of GIC Private Limited, the wealth fund of Singapore.

I have not read such a clear analysis of the function of leadership written so succinctly and in such practical terms. It should be on the required reading list of university courses not only in Singapore, but major universities everywhere."

Professor Chan Heng Chee
Chairman, Lee Kuan Yew Centre for Innovative Cities
Singapore University of Technology and Design
Singapore

"The Leader, the Teacher and You makes us aware that what we do is not just for ourselves, but also for future generations. It is full of a wisdom born of a vast experience and a propensity to take the long view, while remaining acutely relevant for the immediate. Siong Guan Lim is the consummate teacher and role-models the title of the book. While there are suggestions on how to skim through selectively, I would encourage readers to read the whole book to get the true gist of the thinking that has helped to make civil servants people that count in our nation."

Mrs Belinda Charles
Dean, Academy of Principals
Singapore

"A remarkable book… after I started reading it I simply couldn't put it down. It has great insights, is fun to read, and deserves to be widely read. It is full of practical wisdom for a wide range of people — from full time mums to business leaders. It sets out a framework for leaders based on values and culture, but also on lessons learned by having to take tough decisions. Siong Guan Lim had an outstanding career in the development of Singapore. The ability, motivation, and vision of the author and his colleagues are clearly one reason why Singapore and Lee Kuan Yew were so successful. Because of this, the book is a great insight to understanding the phenomenon of Singapore."

Lord Griffiths of Fforestfach
Vice Chairman, Goldman Sachs International
United Kingdom

"Siong Guan Lim has led and managed at the most senior levels of the Singaporean government. Any leader would love to have him at his/her side, advising, counselling, provoking, and reminding. We cannot have him with us in person, but we do have this book that extracts the lessons that he has garnered from his many years of experience. We are fortunate that he has chosen to share his wisdom in writing.

I have used some of his wisdom in my Harvard Kennedy School course on Effective Implementation for more than ten years. It has stood the test of time. Now, with the advent of the book, I will borrow even more from him. My students and I are grateful."

Mr Francis Hartmann
Adjunct Lecturer in Public Policy and Originator of the Kennedy School Course on Effective Implementation, Harvard Kennedy School of Government United States of America

"Academics often think of themselves as being like monks in a monastery, each person being responsible only for themselves and advancing their own careers. This book by Siong Guan Lim shows what real leadership can do to collectively achieve far more than can be done individually.

This book contains the lessons and reflections of an outstanding practitioner of the art of leadership. Siong Guan Lim served in many senior positions of the Singapore Civil Service with great distinction and effectiveness. The fact that he was moved repeatedly from one senior position to another is a testament to his ability. In a society dedicated to promotion on the basis of merit, he was clearly meritorious.

The book contains many important lessons and challenges based on what the author has learned and practiced himself. As he points out himself, the true testament of a leader is to look at what remains after he is gone. By that measure he did exceptionally well since the Singaporean public service and Ministry of Defence are models of efficiency and effectiveness. He points out that organizations need to change in good times and in good time so that they are not overtaken by the future. He clearly succeeded in the ones that he ran. I trust that the current leadership in these organizations will take his lessons to heart.

Relative to other books I have read on leadership, this is one of the best. It is full of practical wisdom, insights and challenges. The focus on values as critical is what I have observed in the organizations I have led. I could not put it down once I started reading it. I would put it as a must read for any leader of an organization of any size. I certainly intend to use it in my leadership challenges."

Professor Daniel Hastings
Cecil and Ida Green Education Professor of Aeronautics and Astronautics and Engineering Systems, Massachusetts Institute of Technology (MIT), and Director/ Chief Executive Officer of Singapore-MIT Alliance for Research and Technology United States of America

"This book is truly unique: it is written and packaged like the numerous self-help books on leadership with tips and challenges, but its objective is not to teach someone how to get ahead and be successful by learning leadership techniques.

At its heart is a simple and yet profound message — that to lead, one has to inspire people to aspire beyond themselves. Messages like 'at the heart of every human being is a desire for meaning and purpose in life' is a call for true values-based leadership, and a selflessness that is reflected by the book's fundamental premise: to be a good leader, one has to be a great teacher.

Through examples from his own very public record of service to the nation and written in a way that is very accessible to young people, Siong Guan Lim is himself a teacher-leader.

The one message that resonates through the book is his observation that 'time passes and people die, but principles and values are what live on.' Young Singaporeans should absorb the book's messages into their daily lives, and by so doing they will become the selfless teacher-leaders, which Siong Guan Lim is the best example of."

Mr Ho Kwon Ping and Ms Claire Chiang
*Founders, Banyan Tree Hotels and Resorts
Singapore*

"We live in a wicked world. The conventional wisdom is that, in order to succeed, one has to be ruthless and unprincipled. Siong Guan Lim's extraordinary success is proof that a man with deep religious convictions and high moral principles can be a successful leader. What is Siong Guan Lim's leadership style? He is a leader with a tough mind and a warm heart, a leader who teaches and develops those who are members of his team. This is a wise and inspiring book."

Professor Tommy Koh
Chairman, Centre for International Law, National University of Singapore
Singapore

"As a life-long student of philosophy, I have been struck how scarce wisdom is in our world, even though it has been revered throughout the ages. This is why Siong Guan Lim's book is special. It is probably one of the wisest books I have read about the Singapore experience. At the same time, its principles have universal applicability. Hence, I have no doubt that every reader will benefit from reading it. And the world will become a better place if his wise insights are universally applied."

Professor Kishore Mahbubani
Dean of the Lee Kuan Yew School of Public Policy, National University of Singapore, and Author of "The Great Convergence: Asia, the West, and the Logic of One World"
Singapore

"Siong Guan Lim's book is a fascinating and uplifting read. He evolves an original exposition on the many facets of leadership from his more than 30 years of distinguished public service to Singapore. I recommend it as essential reading for managers be they placed in the private or public sector. Of greatest relevance to me personally was 'Part I: The Teacher' culminating in the chapter on 'Culture and Values' — valuable for those of us leading organisational change and development. Siong Guan's conviction that today's challenges demand values-driven solutions resonates sharply and persuasively. This book is organised to lovingly teach you how to lead yourself and your people to be the best that everyone can be."

Mr Philip Ng
Chief Executive Officer, Far East Organization, and Chairman of the Singapore University of Technology and Design Board of Trustees
Singapore

"An extensive collection of great quotations and life principles by Siong Guan Lim has provided me with personal inspiration and valuable professional insights as a CEO of a company whose continued success depends on its people. As every principle is intelligently articulated, reading this book will surely motivate and encourage all leaders."

Mr Takeshi Niinami
Chief Executive Officer of Lawson, Inc.
Japan

"*The Leader, The Teacher & You: Leadership Through The Third Generation* is a reflective account on teacher leadership by Siong Guan Lim, a former top civil servant with an illustrious career. Unlike many other books on the subject, he imparts thoughtful advice and perceptive lessons on leadership through easy to understand anecdotes and quotes from distinguished leaders such as Singapore's founding fathers Mr Lee Kuan Yew and the late Dr Goh Keng Swee. This is an essential read for anyone looking to make a positive impact in the lives of others, regardless of age, background, or occupation. His advice is applicable to people from all walks of life, whether one is a civil servant, a business leader or a student."

Dr Stephen Riady
Executive Chairman, OUE Limited
Singapore

"This book captures much of what is important in life from a leadership perspective. Having lived in Singapore and having been a regular visitor since the early 1990's, I have added much to my understanding of why the country has been so successful. A country run by leaders at all levels who exhibit the aspects of great leadership captured here, who really are 'catalysts for change,' and who never stop trying to be the best they can be, has every reason to be successful… and this works in the private sector too!"

Mr John G. Rice
Vice Chairman, General Electric, and
President & Chief Executive Officer of GE Global Growth and Operations
United States of America

"This is an extraordinarily valuable book. Siong Guan Lim and Joanne Lim have managed to do the unusual, which is to create a narrative that is both educational and readable. The writers have elegantly drawn out important experiences and learnings from Siong Guan's long and varied career, and have made them memorable. But this is more than a story of a remarkable career and personal journey but the context, the development of a country whose primary asset is its people, means that the insights are endorsed by the success of a nation."

Sir John Rose
Chairman, Holdingham Group, and
former Chief Executive Officer, Rolls Royce Inc.
United Kingdom

"One of the most insightful books in German literature is the novel *The Buddenbrooks of Thomas Mann*. It describes the decline of a family. Again and again looking at dynasties or business houses, we witness the seemingly unavoidable descent from great heights of success to failure. How can this be prevented? The answer is selfless and competent leadership! The young look for role models and guidance, which can only be provided by elders who by their achievements and their life show them that there are lofty goals worth striving for. Read this book for ideas and ideals."

Mr Urs Schoettli
Consultant on Asian Affairs and former Asia Correspondent of
Neue Zürcher Zeitung (Switzerland) in Beijing, Hong Kong, Delhi, and Tokyo

"Siong Guan Lim has been at the helm of many organizations critical in the transformation of Singapore into an economic powerhouse, from the civil service to the Economic Development Board to GIC, the fund manager for Singapore's foreign reserves. As autobiographical as it is motivational, *The Leader, the Teacher, and You* is a must-read for executives, public servants, and students of East Asian development. Yet the wisdom of its general insights, as well as the humility with which they are delivered, will be an inspiration for any reader."

Dr Toni Schönenberger
Chief Executive Officer, UBS Wolfsberg, and Chairman, stars Foundation Board
Switzerland

"The transformation of Singapore has often been credited to the leadership of its succession of Prime Ministers. However, behind them are other leaders who do the actual grunt work and make things happen. This book tells the remarkable story of one such man, Siong Guan Lim, the son of a taxi driver, starting his career as a sewerage engineer and rising to be the Head of the Civil Service, having served as Principal Private Secretary to the Prime Minister, as well as Permanent Secretary for the Defence, Education, and Finance Ministries along the way. And today he sits as Group President of one of the largest global sovereign wealth funds. There are fascinating insights into the way he led innovative changes in the government departments he served. After three decades, there are countless nuggets of wisdom here for us to learn from. There are many things that I admire about Siong Guan — his appetite for learning, courage to accept new appointments, his ability to lead wholesale management changes, and so on. But most of all I admire his humility, his empathy, and his ability to encourage and inspire others to do the best they can. Reading his story made me wish I had worked for such a leader and mentor."

Dato Dr Kim Tan
Chairman, SpringHill Management Ltd.
United Kingdom

"Siong Guan Lim was Head of the well-known Singapore Civil Service. His book is full of aphorisms that are aimed primarily at the empowerment of people in a large complex organization and the role of an enlightened leadership. He ends the book with a quote from Laozi — 'As for the best leaders, people do not notice their existence.' The entire civil service of Singapore could do very well for themselves, but more importantly for Singaporeans, by taking a refresher course through reading this book. Civil servants today must take the risks of constructive change. The lessons of the book could prevent the stasis that dominant ruling parties undergo as witnessed with the KMT in Taiwan and the LDP in Japan."

Dr Tommy Tan
Chief Executive Officer, TC Capital
Singapore

"One learns how to do something, but one can also do in order to learn. This is a book by a dedicated Singapore civil servant who did both by following able leaders who were also great teachers. Drawing lessons from a lifetime's work, he offers advice to all those who wish to succeed in serving their society with integrity."

Professor Wang Gungwu
Chairman of the East Asian Institute and University Professor
National University of Singapore
Singapore

"This book was written by my good friend Siong Guan Lim based on his observations and experience in his public career since 1969. It reflects his lifestyle, wisdom, life, and beliefs. With keen insight, he describes the behaviour of human groups, for example, by using the image of GEESE in a thoughtful and persuasive way.

While each society may need a slightly different type of leader, there are some basic requirements that make a superior leader. Some leaders, while they are leading their people, are brilliant and exemplary with a clear vision for the future. But once they leave, the group may face an abrupt slowdown or even chaos. Siong Guan clearly states that such leaders are not the best ones. Not leading from the front, nor from the side, nor from behind, but 'from within' is what makes the best leader, he writes. There is so much truth in his statement that the leader must seek to be like the teacher, where the true measure of success is how well the student can surpass the teacher.

Siong Guan and I are involved in sharing ideas on lessons for leaders of the future generation. I find his thoughts and contributions to be highly original and instructive."

Mr Hiroshi Watanabe
Chief Executive Officer/ Executive Managing Director
Japan Bank for International Co-operation
Japan

"Siong Guan Lim has written an outstanding book, and he has done this because he is an outstanding man. Lim has been on the frontlines of Singapore's rapid development over the past forty years providing vital leadership in defence, education, finance, the Prime Minister's Office, and as Head of the Civil Service. He captures the leadership lessons from his mentors — some of the founding fathers of Singapore — and the leadership lessons born of direct experience building a world-class public service. Few practitioners in the art of leadership and governance have had the experience that Lim has had, and few would be able to reflect on that experience and generate such an amazing guidebook for anyone serious about leadership and change. If you want to raise your institution, your government, or your nation to the next level of performance, then this book is for you."

Mr Dean Williams
Lecturer in Public Policy, Center for Public Leadership
Harvard Kennedy School of Government
United States of America

"The dearth in courageous moral leadership in our world today has left many political and economic institutions weakened and compromised. In this book, Siong Guan offers us tried and tested truths on leadership that he personally embodied throughout his time with the Singaporean Government Civil Service, Economic Development Board, and GIC. We have much to learn from him!"

Tan Sri Dr Francis Yeoh
Managing Director, YTL Group of Companies
Malaysia

"An invaluable guide to the heart, soul, and guts of leadership from that rarest of breeds: a true Servant Leader who, in the words of Singapore's Prime Minister, 'established an unbroken record of understanding Singapore's challenges and developing a vision of how the Public Service should respond to these challenges' over an outstanding, 44-year career directly managing key areas of our nation's tumultuous and miraculous transformation.

Having worked under his teacher-leader mentorship, I can testify to both the personal genuineness and organisational effectiveness of Mr Lim's remarkable mastery of that most difficult of management arenas: leading excellence, innovation, and change from the front as a boss, from the side as a comrade, from behind as a mentor, and finally from within as a lasting source of inspiration."

Mr Yeoh Lam Keong
Social Commentator and former GIC Chief Economist
Singapore

APPRECIATION

APPRECIATION

We are all connected in this world: who we are is shaped by our interactions with those who cross our path. The thoughts and ideas behind this book would not have been possible without the contributions and interjections of everyone that I have met. I believe that our interfaces have not been accidents but are part of a divine program under our Creator, who has been and who is the centre of my life.

Particularly for this book, I would like to extend my appreciation to

- **Mr Lee Kuan Yew**, founding Prime Minister of Singapore, and the late **Dr Goh Keng Swee**, former First Deputy Prime Minister of Singapore, who have been the greatest teachers in my working life.
- **Professor Kishore Mahbubani**, for his manifold advice and assistance in connecting the dots that have resulted in this book.
- **The Singapore Public Service Division (PSD) of the Prime Minister's Office** for granting permission to reproduce my past contributions to its Challenge Magazine, which are reproduced throughout this book as "challenges."

I would also like to thank the following leaders who have taken the time to review the book and provide their reactions:

- **Senator Bill Bradley**, Former U.S. Senator and a Managing Director at Allen & Co., United States of America
- **Mrs Belinda Charles**, Dean, Academy of Principals, Singapore
- **Professor Chan Heng Chee**, Chairman, Lee Kuan Yew Centre for Innovative Cities, Singapore University of Technology and Design, Singapore
- **Ms Claire Chiang**, Founder, Banyan Tree Hotels and Resorts, Singapore
- **Lord Griffiths of Fforestfach**, Vice Chairman, Goldman Sachs International, United Kingdom

- **Mr Francis Hartmann**, Adjunct Lecturer in Public Policy and Originator of the Kennedy School Course on Effective Implementation, Harvard Kennedy School of Government, United States of America

- **Professor Daniel Hastings**, Cecil and Ida Green Education Professor of Aeronautics and Astronautics and Engineering Systems, Massachusetts Institute of Technology (MIT), and Director/Chief Executive Officer of Singapore-MIT Alliance for Research and Technology, United States of America

- **Mr Ho Kwon Ping**, Founder, Banyan Tree Hotels and Resorts, Singapore

- **Professor Tommy Koh**, Chairman, Centre for International Law, National University of Singapore, Singapore

- **Professor Kishore Mahbubani**, Dean of the Lee Kuan Yew School of Public Policy, National University of Singapore, and Author of *The Great Convergence: Asia, the West, and the Logic of One World*, Singapore

- **Mr Philip Ng**, Chief Executive Officer, Far East Organization, and Chairman of the Singapore University of Design and Technology Board of Trustees, Singapore

- **Mr Takeshi Niinami**, Chief Executive Officer of Lawson, Inc., Japan

- **Dr Stephen Riady**, Executive Chairman, OUE Limited, Singapore

- **Mr John Rice**, Vice Chairman of General Electric and President & CEO of GE Global Growth and Operations, United States of America

- **Sir John Rose**, Chairman, Holdingham Group, and former CEO, Rolls Royce Inc., United Kingdom

- **Mr Urs Schoettli**, Consultant on Asian Affairs and former Asia Correspondent of Neue Zürcher Zeitung (Switzerland) in Beijing, Hong Kong, Delhi, and Tokyo

- **Dr Toni Schönenberger**, Chief Executive Officer, UBS Wolfsberg and Chairman, stars Foundation Board, Switzerland

- **Dato Dr Kim Tan**, Chairman, SpringHill Management Ltd., United Kingdom

- **Dr Tommy Tan**, Chief Executive Officer, TC Capital, Singapore
- **Professor Wang Gungwu**, Chairman of the East Asian Institute and University Professor, National University of Singapore, Singapore
- **Mr Hiroshi Watanabe**, Chief Executive Officer/Executive Managing Director, Japan Bank for International Co-operation, Japan
- **Mr Dean Williams**, Lecturer in Public Policy, Center for Public Leadership, Harvard Kennedy School of Government, United States of America
- **Tan Sri Dr Francis Yeoh**, Managing Director, YTL Corporation, Malaysia
- **Mr Yeoh Lam Keong**, Social Commentator and former GIC Chief Economist, Singapore

Siong Guan Lim
January 2014

CONTENTS

CHALLENGES

Dedicated with love to
my bride, Jennifer,
my mother, Mary,
and my sister, Violet,
in whom I saw that
the heart of the teacher is different.

Siong Guan Lim, January 2014, Singapore

青出于蓝胜于蓝

**The true mark of success for a teacher is
when one's student surpasses one's self.
It should be no different for a leader.**

富不过三代

"Wealth does not last beyond three generations,"
unless there is a codification of values and principles of
successful leadership, and a regular re-expression of the values
and principles in ways relevant to each generation.

PREFACE

15 September 2006

Mr Lim Siong Guan
Permanent Secretary
Ministry of Finance

Dear Siong Guan,

As you will be retiring from the Administrative Service on 1 October 2006, I wish to record the Government's appreciation for your sterling contributions in the Public Service over the past 37 years.

You have served as Permanent Secretary in several key ministries – the Ministry of Defence, the Prime Minister's Office, the Ministry of Education and the Ministry of Finance. You were also Head, Civil Service from 1999 to 2005.

Throughout your career, you have established an unbroken record of understanding Singapore's challenges and developing a vision of how the Public Service should respond to these challenges. You have turned this vision into strategic ideas and programmes, and seen through their successful implementation. Under your leadership, the Singapore Public Service has become more forward looking, responsive to change, performance-driven and customer-focused. It is admired and respected by countries worldwide.

As Permanent Secretary (Prime Minister's Office) and subsequently Head of Civil Service, you pushed the Public Service constantly to act in time for the future. You established and championed the PS21 *(Public Service for the 21st century)* movement which galvanised public officers at all levels to anticipate change, welcome change and execute change. You restructured the personnel management system, made the Service more competitive and responsive to the changing employment landscape, and introduced policies to attract and develop talent so as to sustain the pipeline of public sector leadership. You have strengthened the spirit of teamwork and collegiality among the Permanent Secretaries, providing the basis for a more networked government.

As Permanent Secretary (Finance), you transformed the government's financial management system. Through innovative initiatives, you incentivised public agencies to strive for excellence, derive the best value for money, and establish clear accountability while limiting fiscal risks to the Government. You promoted E-Government, which consistently ranks highly in international surveys, and is well utilized by the public. You also led the Ministry to reduce income tax rates and enhance Singapore's tax competitiveness, while maintaining a sound fiscal position.

As Permanent Secretary (Education), you were the architect of the *Thinking Schools, Learning Nation* initiative. You spearheaded the introduction of National Education in schools. You built up pride in the teaching profession through measures such as the Principals' Investiture Ceremony and the President's Award for Teachers. At the Ministry of Defence, you built up a strong and credible SAF, staffed by able officers at every level. Through MINDEF's Productivity Committee, you motivated officers at all levels to improve their work. You cultivated, expanded and strengthened our defence relations with key countries. The high public standing of the SAF today is due in no small part to the strong foundations you laid at MINDEF.

Officers who have worked with you respect you as a teacher, mentor and developer of people. They attest to your genuine concern for people and your ability to draw out the best from them. You have pushed for what you believe in, communicated with passion, enthusiasm and sincerity, and inspired an entire generation of younger officers to serve and excel.

I have been privileged to know and work with you for more than three decades, through various stages of your career in MINDEF, PMO and MOF. I have always valued greatly your insights, wisdom and judgement. You exemplify the best traditions of the Administrative Service. I thank you for your dedicated service, and look forward to your continued contributions in the public sector as Chairman of the Economic Development Board.

With best wishes,

Yours sincerely,

Lee Hsien Loong

cc   Head, Civil Service

INTRODUCTION

At the heart of every human being is a desire for meaning and purpose in life.

There is nothing that gives each of us more happiness than to know that we have been useful and helpful to another person.

You can make a difference to the lives around you.

Your life counts.

HOW THIS BOOK CAME ABOUT

This book is part biography, part commentary, and part exposition. It is a book born out of a desire to share ideas derived from my thoughts and practices in the belief that the fullest test of leadership lies in being able to successfully raise the next generation of leaders who live the values of the founding fathers, and who exercise continual rethinking in changing circumstances to achieve sustained success.

If you should learn just one thing that enhances your life, this book will have achieved its purpose. May you have the desire to lead, the humility to learn, the fortitude to strive, and the joy of being able to help and encourage another life within your sphere of influence.

WHO THIS BOOK IS FOR

This book is for anyone who wants to positively influence others around them. You could be a CEO of a multi-national corporation, a stay-at-home mother, an emergency room nurse, or a secondary school student. The fact is that your life counts and you have the potential to be a thought leader and influencer in your own right.

I believe that at the heart of every human being is a desire for meaning and purpose in life. Different people seek different ways to discover that purpose, but many people testify that nothing beats contributing to the lives of other human beings.

There is nothing that gives each of us more happiness than to know we have been useful and helpful to another person — that person might be our parents, our spouse, our children, our colleagues at work, our neighbours, or even strangers we meet on the street. A word of thanks, a smile of gratitude, and/or a gesture of appreciation does something to the heart that money cannot do.

WHAT THIS BOOK IS ABOUT

This book is a reflection of what I learned from my teachers: people I served under, such as Mr Lee Kuan Yew (the first Prime Minister of Singapore) and Dr Goh Keng Swee (once the First Deputy Prime

You may not agree with all the points in this book — that will not only be fine, but necessary, as ideas must always be put together in a way that makes sense within the context of time and circumstance.

May you be able to glean insights and principles from these pages that will give you the courage to:

- Think independently
- Seek to develop capabilities unique to yourself
- Aspire to be number one in the way you think and act, driven always to be in time for the future

Minister of Singapore), people I served with, people who served me, people who wrote articles and books that inspired me, and the many who have touched me in some way.

I will share with you the best ideas I have come across and the convictions I have espoused over the course of my career. You may not agree with all the points in this book — that will not only be fine, but necessary, as ideas must always be put together in a way that makes sense within the context of time and circumstance. Please be assured that these are not thoughts developed in vacuum, but ideas and ideals borne out of practice and experience.

What I hope is that you will be able to glean insights and principles from these pages that will give you the courage to think independently, to seek to develop capabilities unique to yourself, and to aspire to be number one in the way you think and act, driven always to be in time for the future.

HOW THIS BOOK IS WRITTEN

This book is written in two parts. In addition, I have included a "challenge" at the end of every chapter, for you to incorporate in your personal and professional life.[1]

The first part, "The Teacher," describes events in my work life that have been learning points for me. In this part of the book, I share the lessons that I have learned from various teachers in my life and through varied experiences in life.

The second part of the book, "The Leader," details my thoughts on leadership within a framework of principles and ideas, and discusses how culture and values build sustainable success for organisations. The chapter entitled "Pursuit of Excellence" describes excellence as a frame of mind to always be the best we can be; "Position Leadership" describes what the leader in an organisation is expected to do well; and "Personal Leadership" makes the point that it is the quality of personal leadership that determines how successful you can be as a leader.

---

[1] These articles are reprinted from Challenge magazine © 2001–2004 Public Service Division (PSD), Prime Minister's Office, and are used by permission of the PSD.

This book posits that the highest aspiration of the leader is to be a true teacher.

The teacher rejoices when the student realises his or her full potential.

The more the student exceeds the teacher, the greater we could consider the success of the teacher to be!

The final section, "The Leader, The Teacher," posits that the highest aspiration of the leader is to be a true teacher. The teacher rejoices when the student realises his or her full potential; indeed, the more the student exceeds the teacher, the greater we could consider the success of the teacher to be!

When I started work in 1969, the world was practically a different world from today, where things move so fast that the future appears more unpredictable and uncertain than ever, and life is a continuous push to stay ahead.

The success of the teacher lies in developing, equipping, and empowering the student to be able to effectively function and live well... well into the future. This also should be how we assess the success of a leader!

HOW TO USE THIS BOOK

We are all different and have different needs. I understand that in a time-starved world, you might like to select the bare minimum to read, to meet your needs as quickly as possible.

- For those who would like to get a rough gist of the book:
    - → Read the quotes on every other page
    - → Read the Challenge section at the end of each chapter
    - → Read the Closing Thoughts

- For Public Officers and those who would like to get insights into the history of the Civil Service in Singapore:
    - → Read Part I: "The Teacher"
    - → Read the Challenge section at the end of each chapter
    - → Read the Closing Thoughts

- For Leaders and those interested in leading into the future:
    - → Read Part II: "The Leader"
    - → Read the Challenge section at the end of each chapter
    - → Read the Closing Thoughts

Today is not more difficult than the past; it is simply different.

Life moves on with all its ebbs and flows, and the key to happiness and success lies with those who are able to live with the ambiguous and the unexpected, as well as with uncomfortable and continuous change.

Each generation has its own issues, its own challenges, and its own opportunities.

Time passes and people die, but principles and values live on.

PRINCIPLES AND VALUES LIVE ON

It is an illusion to think that today is more difficult than the past; it is simply different. Life moves on with all its ebbs and flows, and the key to happiness and success lies with those who are able to live with the ambiguous and the unexpected, as well as with uncomfortable and continuous change.

When I left to study mechanical engineering at the University of Adelaide in early 1965, Singapore had left behind its colonial past and merged with Malaysia for just over a year. But only months later, Singapore was no longer a part of Malaysia. Things could not have been more uncertain, unexpected, and uncomfortable, but it was a world that young people today cannot be blamed for not being able to feel or sense.

Each generation has its own issues, its own challenges, and its own opportunities. Time passes and people die, but principles and values live on. The applications have to fit the context to create a worthy tomorrow.

From where does the power come for leaders to stretch beyond themselves? Each of us must find our own answer. I can only describe mine.

As you read this book, please keep in mind that while the gathering of ideas is a smart thing to do, success lies in putting good ideas together in a systemic whole that results in different, innovative, and unique ideas. Too often we ask others, "What do you do, and how do you do it?" Too seldom do we ask, "Why do you think that way and why do you do it like that?"

I hope this book will help you positively influence the people around you to do good, to excel, and above all, to build upon the past today so that we all can be in time for the future.

CHALLENGE 1

BE YOURSELF

Charles Handy wrote a story at the end of his book, "The Empty Raincoat":

"There was a rabbi once, called Zuzya of Hannipol. He spent his life lamenting his lack of talent and his failure to be another Moses. One day, God comforted him. 'In the coming world,' he said, 'we will not ask you why you were not Moses, but why you were not Zuzya.'"

Each of us should try to be the best that we can be according to what we are able to do.

We can attend courses so that we know more things. We can learn from other people so that we can do better. Each person must not be satisfied with himself until he is the best that he can be.

Do not compare yourself with others. Simply be the best that you can be, and do the best you can.

If you are already the best that you can be, and you are already doing your best, then no one has the right to ask you for more. But if you are not putting in your best, then you should be angry with yourself.

Allow me to share with you a poem simply called *Youth* by Samuel Ullman. This was the favourite poem of Konosuke Matsushita, the founder of Matsushita Electric Corporation, which makes electrical goods for brands such as Panasonic and National.

While some of the words of the poem may not be easy to understand, I think the message is simple and clear. I hope the poem will inspire you, just as it has been an encouragement in my life.

It goes:

"Youth is not a time of life;
it is a state of mind;
it is not a matter of rosy cheeks, red lips and supple knees;
it is a matter of the will, a quality of the imagination,
a vigour of the emotions;
it is the freshness of the deep springs of life.
Youth means a temperamental predominance of courage over
timidity, of the appetite for adventure over the love of ease.
This often exists in a man of sixty more than a boy of twenty.
Nobody grows old merely by a number of years.
We grow old by deserting our ideals."

May we all keep alive the spirit of youth in our lives — the spirit that moves each of us to be the best we can be.

PART I

THE TEACHER

CHAPTER 1

Walk the ground!

Do not sit in the office without getting to know the people on the ground and seeing the true situation on the ground for yourself.

If people see your willingness to get your hands dirty, they will respect you for taking the time and effort to understand their situation.

Chapter 1

MY TEACHERS

It was a bright, sunny morning in July 1969. I was reporting for my first day of work at a sewage treatment plant. As I drove through the main gate, I noticed a couple of men painting a road roller that obviously had not been used for some time.

Once in the office, I asked why the road roller was being painted the normal grey of such equipment; I was told it was because the road roller was being "condemned" — a term used to describe the retirement of the equipment so a replacement could be bought.

The answer deepened the mystery. Why spend the effort to paint a piece of equipment that was being discarded?

"Oh," one of the men explained, "the 'certificate of condemnation' has to be signed by an engineer from the Public Works Department. If he saw the rusting equipment, he would say we caused the equipment's sorry state because we did not take care of it."

In other words, the men had left the irreparable piece of equipment in the rain; then after a decent interval, they painted it up so they would not get blamed for the state of disrepair. This way, everyone wins — the engineer would not cast blame and would be fully justified in issuing the "condemnation certificate," and the workers could look forward to a new machine.

This taught me a very important lesson: The people on the ground are much smarter than you think… so walk the ground! Do not sit in the office without getting to know the people on the ground and seeing the true situation on the ground for yourself. If people see your willingness to get your hands dirty, they will respect you for taking the time and effort to understand their situation.

Be there for the troops!

People want:

- To be appreciated
- To have their work acknowledged
- To taste success

The challenge for leaders is how to create situations where:

- People are not afraid to try
- People can savour success to build up their self-confidence
- People can safely learn from their mistakes

The lesson about being on the ground and being there for the "troops" was brought home forcefully to me when massive floods occurred in Singapore a few months after I started work at the sewage treatment plant as a mechanical engineer. I was also responsible for the mechanical and electrical installations at various sewage pumping stations.

The water was overflowing the riverbanks and submerged the massive pumps at one of the stations. We had to get the water out of the basement where the pumps were located before the massive pumps could be restarted. When I arrived on the scene, the workers were already strenuously at work trying to get the water out with a few mobile diesel-driven pumps, but the mobile pumps were simply not up to the task.

I told the workers to link the pumps together to get more suction power. They told me this had never been done before, which immediately put me in a mental quandary as to whether what I was asking them to do was sound. I quickly recollected in my mind what I had been taught in university about hydraulics, and told the workers to push on with the idea. Fortunately, things worked out, and I sensed my standing in the eyes of the workers went up several notches.

After many years of working with people, I have uncovered a host of universal characteristics about people. People have a deep sense of pride and want to do a good job. People want to be appreciated and want their work to be acknowledged. People want to taste success, and when they do, they automatically become more motivated and more self-confident, which in turn engenders initiative and innovation. No one wants to look stupid or fail on their job.

The challenge for leaders is how to create situations where people are not afraid to try, where people can savour success to build up their self-confidence, and where people can safely learn from their mistakes.

More fundamentally, I have learned that most people want to be led; what they seek are good leaders who work with both their head and heart, and who will help their people discover themselves. Good leaders are for their people both a shepherd and a teacher, and serve to guide their people, empathise with them, energise them, synergise their work, and embolden them to think innovatively and act courageously.

I served in the Singapore Civil Service for 37 years, from 1969 to 2006. Throughout my career, my starting position has always been to seek to be

We must always seek to be Number One in our thinking.

We must think for ourselves and seek to develop capabilities unique to ourselves.

We must be prepared to learn from everywhere, but we must always be clear why we are doing what we are doing.

Above all, we must be comfortable to be in front where there is no one else to follow and we are making our own way.

leaders in our thinking, not followers. We might be ranked number two or even fifty rather than Number One in the ranking table, but what must set us apart is that we think for ourselves and seek to develop capabilities unique to ourselves. We must be prepared to learn from everywhere, but we must always be clear why we are doing what we are doing. We must be comfortable following, but above all, we must be comfortable to be in front where there is no one else to follow and we are making our own way. This is what makes the difference between being Number One and not being number one; it is the difference between sustaining success and degrading performance in an unknowable future.

Allow me to illustrate my point by comparing riding an escalator to climbing the stairs. The people who simply stand on the escalator will feel inadequate when they reach a level where there is no escalator but only a staircase to go to the next level — they have never developed the muscles to give them the strength, energy, and confidence to climb the stairs. So using the escalator is a good idea: ride on what others are doing, but walk up the escalator at the same time to develop your muscles and capability as you go!

I have often been asked who I had learnt the most from and who had helped form my thoughts on leadership. I always answer without hesitation that they were Mr Lee Kuan Yew, the first Prime Minister of Singapore, and Dr Goh Keng Swee, the former First Deputy Prime Minister of Singapore.

People often ask me what it was like to serve Mr Lee Kuan Yew, as he was known to be very tough and demanding of high standards of work. They always react with surprise when I tell them that the three years as his Principal Private Secretary were the freest three years of my working life!

In all my other career appointments, I could determine the agenda for thought and action, so my diary was continually full as there was always more that could be done in improvement and innovation than there was time and people to drive the change. However, when I was serving Mr Lee Kuan Yew, I could only operate within his agenda, and thus I had time on my hands to read books and think deeply about issues of life and the government of nations.

From Mr Lee, I learnt the principles of governance that undergirded the transformation of Singapore from the early days of self-government

Building a nation is not the same as building a city: a city is made of plans and concrete structures, but a nation is made of people united to work together for a bright future for all.

A leader needs to have:

- Clarity of views
- Single-mindedness of purpose
- A capacity for clear communication

in 1959, subsequent independence in 1965, and her development and evolution into a modern metropolis.

Mr Lee taught me that building a nation is not the same as building a city: a city is made of plans and concrete structures, but a nation is made of people united to work together for a bright future for all. Mr Lee also taught me that a leader not only needs to have clarity of views and single-mindedness of purpose, but also requires a capacity for clear communication, where complex problems are conveyed in a way that can be understood by the man-in-the-street.

I well remember my first meeting with Mr Lee as his Principal Private Secretary. He told me that in the course of my work, I would be dealing with foreigners, and advised, "Always look the foreigner in his eyes. Never look down. You are dealing with him as a representative of Singapore. Conduct yourself as his equal." As I look back, I plainly see that in this wise instruction lies the reason for what has made Singapore so much of what it is — well-regarded by the world, respected, self-aware, pushing always against the boundaries of possibilities.

From Dr Goh Keng Swee, I learnt the art of getting things done in situations of ambiguity and uncertainty. I learnt the importance to have the courage to try new things and the discernment to cut losses when things do not work out. I learnt to think clearly and never to camouflage ambiguity and uncertainty with words. I learnt the need to set goals that are a stretch but achievable with effort and imagination. I learnt how to harness the energies of people to a high and worthy cause. I learnt the need to be open to good ideas from anywhere, and to have an indomitable spirit to be masters of our own destiny. Above all, I learnt from Dr Goh that "the only way to avoid making mistakes is not to do anything, and that, in the final analysis, will be the ultimate mistake."

Lee Kuan Yew and Goh Keng Swee were master teachers to me, and even though they might not have realised it, they infused deep lessons on leadership and governance in my soul. From them, I learnt always to be on the lookout for talent and to do whatever I can to allow people to achieve their potential.

Mr Lee and Dr Goh also impressed on me the need for Singaporeans to have a relentless drive for excellence, and desire to be the best that we can be in everything we do; for Singapore, unlike for so many other

Singaporeans need to have a relentless drive for excellence, and desire to be the best that we can be in everything we do.

For Singapore, survival and success are two sides of the same coin. No one owes us a living and no one else is responsible for our security.

The drive to be exceptional in the way we think is not an option; it is destiny for Singapore.

Success only comes with the apt application of principles that fit the context of time and circumstance, and is fired by the human spirit that says tomorrow can be better than today.

countries, survival and success are two sides of the same coin. There are countries that are independent but not sovereign, and countries that are sovereign but not independent. Singapore must seek to be friends with all who would be friends with Singapore, but never forget that no one owes us a living and that no one else is responsible for our security. The drive to be exceptional in the way we think is not an option; it is destiny for Singapore.

Throughout my career, I have been blessed with opportunities to make a difference in every place I was at, by offering people a vision and a deep sense of purpose in their work so that they would stretch themselves to the maximum and create the destiny of the nation:

- At the Ministry of Defence, the vision was to lift the morale of the SAF with a public campaign that positioned the soldiers as the "defenders of the nation."
- At the Prime Minister's Office, the vision was to build a public service that was "among the best in the world."
- At the Ministry of Education, the vision was to support teachers and schools as they worked hard to "mould the future of the nation."
- At the Ministry of Finance, the vision was for staff to direct funds towards "creating the Singapore we want."
- At the Economic Development Board, the vision was to "create the economic future for Singapore."
- At GIC, it is to "invest for the future of Singapore."

In every one of these assignments, I have found that people are willing to commit their time and effort, and to go out of their way to put in extra energy and imagination, if the cause at hand is worthy of their efforts and if their contributions are recognised and appreciated. However, success only comes with the apt application of principles that fit the context of time and circumstance, and is fired by the human spirit that says tomorrow can be better than today.

From where does the power come for leaders to stretch beyond themselves? Each of us must find our own answer... I can only describe mine in the following chapters.

CHALLENGE 2

BE THE BEST THAT YOU CAN BE

If I were to offer just one piece of advice to anyone newly starting work, it would simply be, "Be the best you can be."

This requires three actions:

- Doing the best you can in whatever you do
- Making it a priority to realise your potential
- Working well with others to accomplish more than working just on your own

"Doing the best you can in whatever you do" means to be never satisfied until you have put your all into any assignment. There needs to be the "intellectual restlessness" — a continual questioning as to whether things could be done in a better way, and whether you could do better things with your time and energy. There needs also to be a "constructive dissatisfaction" — an unwillingness to be satisfied until the best possible has been done, but an unwillingness that manifests itself in a constructive rather than destructive, sceptical, complaining, or cynical way.

"Making it a priority to realise your potential" means taking every opportunity to improve yourself. It is a willingness to learn, a willingness to accept criticism, a willingness to listen, and a willingness to try new things.

I am saddened when I hear someone say, "I don't see why I should do this when they are not paying me more." That is how we miss opportunities to become better, stretch our abilities, and learn how much more capable we can be. You are being paid with opportunity, if not with money.

Separate the matter of pay from the willingness to do more. If you are not prepared to do more, you will miss the chance to establish your credentials to be entrusted with more. And if you do more but do not get the promotion or recognition in due time, you always have a choice to go somewhere else where your skill and experience will be given adequate recognition.

There is no need to stay where you are and be miserable. At the same time, the only one who loses by not stretching himself or herself is you.

"Working well with others to accomplish more than working just on your own" means recognising there are very few things in work and life that you can do all on your own; it is thus important to develop networks and nurture relationships. Synergy and symbiosis guarantee greater achievement than "flying solo." Learn to "put yourself in the other person's shoes," and to "do unto others as you would have them do unto you." There has to be self-confidence, but there has to be humility too. Share with others, and together make things happen.

Living these three precepts in the public service is not difficult if you are willing. The mission is honourable — to serve Singaporeans and Singapore. It lives on meritocracy, offers opportunity to contribute and to try, and naturally demands working not just within a department but also across agencies.

"Be the best you can be" is good for your advancement, your sense of self-worth, your enhancement of knowledge and experience, and your ability to contribute. It is good for your soul.

CHAPTER 2

There is always something new to learn in every situation.

If you keep choosing what you want to do, you will be confining yourself to the world you know, and might miss the opportunity to learn things that you never imagined you could!

Chapter 2

OPPORTUNITIES AND OBLIGATIONS

My father was a taxi driver, and my mother was a teacher. There was no way I could have gone to university without a scholarship.

In the 1960s, scholarships, bursaries and loans were a lot scarcer than they are today. I applied for several scholarships and was awarded the Colombo Plan Scholarship that was generously donated by the Australian Government and awarded by the Singapore Public Service Commission.

Unlike today where young people can pick, choose, and even demand what they want to study, I was prepared to do any course they were prepared to give me a scholarship for. I studied mechanical engineering because that was the offer for a scholarship, those being the early days of industrialisation in Singapore.

When I returned with an obligation to serve in the Singapore Civil Service for a number of years, I was posted to the Sewerage Branch of the Public Works Department, now the Public Utilities Board. I can tell you it was not the most pleasant of assignments, breathing and managing the systems that handle human wastes in a "more civilised" way. You might think that I was miserable but I was not, as it was a whole new world of experiences.

I believe there is always something new to learn in every situation. Some things you can master in three months, others you can master in three years, and yet there are some things that you can never master even in 30 years! I think that if you keep choosing what you want to do, you will be confining yourself to the world you know, and might miss the opportunity to learn things that you never imagined you could!

Through all my appointments, curiosity and a desire to learn

Chase the Opportunities, not the Rewards!

With opportunities come obligations: the obligation to contribute to those around us, and the obligation to offer others opportunities to discover themselves.

Opportunity comes to those who are able, ready, and prepared.

Enjoy today! But work hard to ensure that your today is better than your yesterday, so that you will have new opportunities tomorrow!

and contribute made up for my lack of technical skills and industrial knowledge. I found that integrity, trustworthiness, reliability, energy, imagination, and a continuous drive for excellence attract to you opportunities to learn, to serve, and to contribute.

Do not chase the rewards! Chase the opportunities. Rewards are what you get for today, while opportunities determine what you get for the future because opportunities govern what you can get to do tomorrow.

I also learned throughout my career that in order to gain the confidence of my staff, I had to convince them I had no desire to steal their credit and I was there purely to facilitate their work, coordinate their efforts, and help them succeed by continually asking the question "How can I help YOU do your job better?"

To garner the energy and creativity of everyone, the leader must never focus on oneself but must always be on the lookout for the good of others. Leadership requires knowledge and experience but, most of all, it must be founded on other-centeredness.

IN CLOSING...

Opportunities are for us to learn and to be the best we each can be. But with opportunities come obligations: the obligation to contribute to those around us, and the obligation to offer others opportunities to discover themselves, just as we have benefitted from the opportunities given to us. In addition, anything less than doing the best that we can and being the best that we can be would be less than fair to ourselves and those around us.

Opportunity comes to those who are able, ready, and prepared. It is important for each one of us to build a reputation for hard work, integrity, trustworthiness, and reliability; our qualifications and achievements today are not the end of our hard work, but the springboard to bigger ends and higher means.

Enjoy today! But work hard to ensure that your today is better than your yesterday, so that you will have new opportunities tomorrow!

BUILD YOUR LIFE WITH PRIDE AND DIGNITY

A very good carpenter felt he was getting old. He informed his boss of his plans to leave.

The boss was sorry to see him go. He asked the carpenter if he could build just one more house as a personal favour.

The carpenter said yes. But after some time it was easy to see he was not trying his best. His workmanship was not good. He used poor materials. It was sad.

The boss came to look at the house when the carpenter finished it. He then gave the carpenter the key to the front door. "This is your house," he said, "my gift to you for so many years of good work."

What a shock! What a shame! If only the carpenter had known he was building his own house, he would have done his job differently. Now he had to live in the home he had not built properly.

There is a lesson in this for all of us. How are we building our lives?

Are we simply following orders or are we doing a good job because we believe any job we do is worth doing well? Are we satisfied when we put in less than our best? Or are we among those who do not give every job their best effort, and then with a shock, they discover that they have to live in the house they were tasked to build. If they had known, I am sure they would have done things differently.

Think of yourself as the carpenter. Think about your house. Build wisely. It is the only life you will ever build. Even if you live for only one more day, that day deserves to be lived with pride and dignity.

Your life today is the result of your attitudes and choices in the past. Your life tomorrow will be the result of your attitudes and the choices you make today.

CHAPTER 3

Mindef itself is somewhat like a mini-government as virtually every function of government can be found in it.

As Mindef was "on its own" finance-wise, it developed unique systems to ensure that it could operate effectively within its allocated "block budget."

Given that threats could arise suddenly, and that major weapon systems took as long as 10 years from first thought to operational capability, it was inherent in Mindef's culture to be able to plan for the future, yet have the capability to respond to unexpected developments.

Chapter 3

LEARNING BY DOING

I served in the Ministry of Defence (Mindef) from 1970 to 1978, and then from 1981 to 1994.[2] The 21 years I spent in Mindef was a remarkable period of learning and experimentation.

Mindef itself is somewhat like a mini-government as virtually every function of government can be found in it. Its annual budget was a "block vote," which meant that the Ministry of Finance funded Mindef without scrutinising the detailed items: Mindef had to figure out for itself how it would manage its capital budget to build camps and buy new weapon systems, and its operating budget to pay for personnel, maintenance, supplies and all other operating costs. This approach avoided any need for Mindef to name potential security threats or war scenarios to justify its budgets, consonant with the belief that if the Singapore Armed Forces (SAF) was well-trained, well-equipped, and well-motivated, deterrence would be effective, military conflict could be avoided, and above all, security and stability could be maintained.

As Mindef was "on its own" finance-wise, it developed unique systems to ensure that it could operate effectively within its allocated "block budget." Given that threats could arise suddenly, and that major weapon systems took as long as 10 years from first thought to operational capability, it was inherent in Mindef's culture to be able to plan for the future, yet have the capability to respond to unexpected developments.

---

[2] From 1971 to 1974, I was the Deputy General Manager of Singapore Automotive Engineering (which later became ST Automotive and then ST Kinetics) for six months before becoming the General Manager. From 1978 to 1981, I served as the Principal Private Secretary to then Prime Minister Lee Kuan Yew.

You do not need to know everything or even anything to undertake a task.

You just need to be willing, able, and prepared to learn.

In fact, consultants have often expressed how remarkably quickly and naturally Mindef officers latch on to tools like scenario planning.

But I have jumped the gun! Let me start from the beginning.

In 1970, after just a year in the Sewerage Branch of the Public Works Department, Dr Goh Keng Swee, then First Deputy Prime Minister and Minister of Defence, chose me together with several others from other government agencies to be transferred to the Ministry of Defence; the build-up of the SAF had to be accelerated significantly as the British had given notice of the withdrawal of their forces East of Suez.

After an appeal to the British Government to delay their withdrawal, Harold Wilson, then the British Prime Minister, gave a few months' respite, but this still meant that the British military establishments would be closed by 1971. The urgency and utmost priority of the task at hand brought Dr Goh back to the Ministry of Defence for the second time in 1970 (Dr Goh first became Defence Minister upon Singapore's independence in August 1965, and had moved on to the Ministry of Finance in 1967).

After I joined Mindef, I was appointed the project director to coordinate the establishment of the first anti-aircraft gun unit of the SAF, the 160 Battalion, then a unit of the Singapore Artillery.

What did I know about anti-aircraft guns? Nothing! But I was prepared to learn. These anti-aircraft guns were Swiss Oerlikon guns with a fire control system from Philips of the Netherlands, and we had Dutch advisors to oversee the build-up as they were familiar with the gun system. My job was to coordinate the various aspects to successfully establish the unit — ensuring that the camp, equipment, and supplies at Seletar would be ready, that the officers and men were trained in good time, that the interface with the Dutch advisors went smoothly, and so on.

I remember turning up at one of the weekly Mindef HQ Meetings, chaired by Dr Goh, with a Critical Path Flowchart of circles, diamonds and arrows drawn on four double-foolscap sheets of paper taped together. I thought it was quite an impressive piece of work, but looking back, it must have seemed to Dr Goh a rather primitive approach! Nevertheless, it must have impressed Dr Goh enough to make me the project director of the Junior Flying Club, now known as the Youth Flying Club, the following year.

Growing the Republic of Singapore Air Force (RSAF) was a matter of utmost priority.

While there were various foreign advisors involved at various times and Dr Goh Keng Swee had many immediate challenges to deal with, he did not overlook building up Singaporean talent where the shortage was greatest, for that would ultimately determine how fast and how much the RSAF would grow.

Dr Goh had the foresight to admit girls for flying training in the Junior Flying Club, even though there was no intention to recruit them as RSAF pilots, because they could influence the thinking of young people, and subsequently their children.

What did I know about planes and flying? Nothing! But I was willing to learn. Dr Goh's idea for setting up the club was to invoke interest in flying among the young, with the hope that they would be inclined to become fighter pilots in the air force when they grow up.

JUNIOR FLYING CLUB

Growing the Republic of Singapore Air Force (RSAF) was a matter of utmost priority. While there were various foreign advisors involved at various times and Dr Goh had many immediate challenges to deal with, he did not overlook building up Singaporean talent where the shortage was greatest, for that would ultimately determine how fast and how much the RSAF would grow.

The Junior Flying Club sought young members from the lower secondary school levels whose interest in aero-modelling could be piqued, and older members at the junior college level who would be trained to attain the Private Pilots' Licence. Dr Goh also had the foresight to admit girls for flying training, even though there was no intention to recruit them as RSAF pilots, because they could influence the thinking of young people, and subsequently their children, about becoming RSAF pilots.

As always, the rule from Dr Goh was to get things moving "faster than was reasonable." Working out of a little, run-down office facility at Empress Place, I started on the Junior Flying Club from scratch, making out the budgets, writing out staff manuals and office procedures, and so on.

As Dr Goh was keen not to spend too much, he decided that instead of training with light aircrafts, we could make do with powered gliders, which are basically gliders that can take off on their own. Together with an advisor who was once a test pilot in the Indian Air Force, I went to Germany and Britain to buy the gliders. We bought them from two places because we wanted to get them in a hurry and get the Junior Flying Club off the ground quickly. The idea of the Junior Flying Club succeeded, with a higher percentage of their members becoming pilots than non-club members, though I have no idea how much of it could be due to pre-selection among students who already had an interest to join the air force.

My two assignments as project director taught me a few things. First,

How to successfully work with experts and people older than you: Convince them that you are there to help them succeed, and not steal their credit.

There are so many interesting things that you can learn if you have the open mind to take on what you know almost nothing about.

I learned how to successfully work with experts and people older than myself by convincing them I was there to help them succeed, and not steal their credit. Second, if you choose what you want to do, you are immediately limiting yourself to what you know you are interested in. There are so many interesting things that you can learn if you have the open mind to take on what you know almost nothing about, just like I knew nothing about anti-aircraft guns or about flying an aircraft.

The Junior Flying Club was my introduction to general management, where I started with the strategic objective set by Dr Goh, but had full freedom to decide what needed to be done and what more could be done. I learnt rudimentary skills in people and financial management, and organisational development. These were skills I had not thought about previously but put me in good stead for my next assignment at Singapore Automotive Engineering.

SINGAPORE AUTOMOTIVE ENGINEERING

The SAF had bought the V200 Armoured Fighting Vehicle, which made up the first Armour unit of the SAF. While basic maintenance of the V200s was carried out at the armour battalion level, higher level maintenance was under the purview of a company, Singapore Automotive Engineering (SAE), which was 100 percent owned by Mindef.

Ten expatriate staff, comprising nine Americans and one British, were employed to get the company going. As the contract for the expatriate staff was coming to an end, a decision had to be made as to whether the leadership of the company should be localised. I was asked if I would like to do it; as I was open for any opportunity to learn, I said yes. Together with another colleague, we went excitedly to SAE. All the expatriates left at the end of their contracts except for two of them, who were willing to work with us.

I entered Singapore Automotive Engineering as the Deputy General Manager for six months, before taking over in the middle of 1972 as the General Manager. Relations with the American General Manager were not that great, as he made no effort to assist with the takeover; but I did not allow this to upset me, and I used the six months to draw up the financial and personnel manuals in preparation for the day when I would be in charge.

Have multiple channels to communicate and engage with your staff.

Towards the end of my six months at SAE, rumours started circulating that the Director of Logistics in Mindef had decided to extend the contract of the expatriates, and that my colleague and I would not be taking over after all. This upset my colleague and me, and we decided to go on strike! We refused to turn up for work at SAE for a couple of days and spent the time with our previous colleagues at Mindef.

The Director of Logistics, who was also the Chairman of the Board of Directors of SAE asked to see us. We felt terrible, and apologised for going on strike, as it was not a right or good thing to do. The Director was most gracious, and told us to get back to the company, which we did, and we took over, I as General Manager, and my colleague as Engineering Manager, on the due date.

I became the General Manager of SAE at the age of 24. Immediately, I saw my challenge to assure cost efficiency and productivity in the company, which had the monopoly of high-level repair and maintenance of the V200 vehicles, and also the overhaul and rebuild of SAF's 3-ton trucks. I decided a good way of controlling costs would be for the company to take on commercial contracts that SAE would need to successfully compete for against competition from other large vehicle workshops in Singapore. This helped lay the foundation for the company's later success as a reputable commercial workshop, while maintaining its unique position as a workshop for the design, production, and overhaul of armoured military vehicles.

One event at SAE, the unionisation of the workshop workers, initially bothered me, though it later turned out to be a positive development. There was no union representation when I joined the company. I had strived to offer fair compensation and a good working environment for the staff, so when the workers decided to be unionised, I felt it somehow reflected a failure on my part. But I later realised that if the workers' union were responsible and responsive, it in fact offered an additional channel for communication and engagement with the workers.

I returned to Mindef after three years at SAE, during which I put in place a Singaporean management that could intuitively identify with the needs and concerns of the Singapore Armed Forces, as well as structures to ensure commercial effectiveness and efficiency.

As things turned out, the timing could not have been more fortuitous.

"The only way to avoid making mistakes is to not do anything. And that, in the final analysis, will be the ultimate mistake!"

Dr Goh Keng Swee

Once you realise you have made a mistake, correct it! The worst thing you can do to your boss and yourself is to surprise your boss with bad news.

We must learn to manage ourselves before we can expect others to trust us.

I was Head of the Engineering Department in the Logistics Division for just a month before I was appointed Director of Logistics at the beginning of 1975. It was an unplanned move, but a welcomingly interesting and challenging one. In fact, so many of my career moves have been unplanned, yet each stage had been so built upon the knowledge and experiences of earlier stages that I am convinced there is an invisible hand and mind behind it all.

I was to be Director of Logistics for just one and a half years before I took on the role of Director of Finance in Mindef, again for just one and a half years. I served under Dr Goh Keng Swee, who was still the Minister of Defence, during these years.

There was a vibrancy, energy, and urgency in Dr Goh's leadership that either incited one to action or cowered one to inaction. No one would last long under Dr Goh who feared to try despite their inexperience and the uncertainties of the time.

What helped me was a very well-known adage of Dr Goh's on mistakes: "The only way to avoid making mistakes is to not do anything. And that, in the final analysis, will be the ultimate mistake!" This quotation was spread all over the SAF in the early days of its formation. It was a call to encourage enterprise, to explore the unknown, to learn from failure, and to inculcate a can-do spirit. This in turn led to the rapid growth of the SAF, the willingness to try new things, the rise of self-confidence, and the gumption to confound cynics and sceptics. It was not, however, an open licence to make mistakes. Dr Goh's rule was: Once you realise you have made a mistake, it is your job to correct it, and if he were likely to learn about the mistake before you had the time to correct it, you had better let him know first!

It is amazing how many people respond to mistakes by simply praying very hard no one will discover it, without realising that the worst thing you can do to your boss and yourself is to surprise your boss with bad news. It is always best for your boss to hear the bad news from you first.

In addition, we must learn to manage ourselves before we can expect others to trust us. Do not allow your ego and fear to impede your capacity to learn, as well as your willingness to try new things. It is foolhardy for any boss to empower a person who is either not competent enough to

"It is better to have stallions, which we occasionally have to pull back, than to have donkeys you have to kick to move."

Dr Goh Keng Swee

Those who expect to harness the power and muscle of stallions must be self-confident, open-minded, intellectually honest, and also humble.

know that things are going wrong, or honest and humble enough to admit that things are going wrong.

To recognise the importance of learning from our mistakes, I introduced an annual award called the "Learning Err-ward" when I became the Permanent Secretary of the Ministry of Finance in later years. This award was given to the person who had found the biggest learning, which in practice amounted to the person who had committed the biggest mistake and learnt from it. The winner was obliged to speak at the rostrum, describe his mistake, share the discovery of, and recovery from, the mistake, and share what lessons were learnt for the future.

Dr Goh had yet another saying: "It is better to have stallions, which we occasionally have to pull back, than to have donkeys you have to kick to move." What Dr Goh looked for was energy, initiative, and imagination. Many supervisors will tell you what they want are people with energy, initiative, and imagination, but in reality, they feel threatened by people who have different views from theirs, and thus discourage or diminish those who carry bad news or make mistakes. Those who expect to harness the power and muscle of stallions must be self-confident, open-minded, intellectually honest, and also humble.

There was a very special lesson I learnt from Dr Goh on the role of staff in an organisation. Dr Goh expected policy papers to be clear and succinct, and that the officer working on a subject would know more than him in that particular area. While Dr Goh might not have agreed with the officer's recommendations, it was very important to him that the officer had thought through the problem.

Dr Goh was intensely curious and loved to ask questions based on the annexes. If the officer could not answer his questions, he would wonder whether he could rely on his or her analyses and recommendations.

During my stint as the Director of Logistics in charge of all the support services and supplies for the army, Mindef was considering a large contract for new trucks. There were three bidders. I recommended that Mindef should buy Truck Model A taking into account the initial cost, expected life, cost of maintenance, and so on. Dr Goh, however, believed that Mindef should buy Truck Model B because he felt the manufacturer was more likely to deliver reliable maintenance support over the long term. Dr Goh called me to his office and explained his views.

A leader should never tell the staff to re-do their analysis, even if they should disagree with their staff's analysis for whatever reason, as they would thereby be undermining their staff's work, their sense of self-worth, and the values of honesty and integrity by telling them to write what they do not believe in.

Allow people to learn from their mistakes.

As a responsive staff officer, I rewrote the submission to recommend Truck Model B, swinging all the arguments to conclude this to be the best recommendation. Dr Goh sent for me again and said he did not want me to change my recommendation to fit his view. He asked me to send back to him my paper making the original recommendation of Truck A. This was no easy task, as those were still the days of the typewriter, not of today's word processor, and I had faithfully torn up the original submission to remove all evidence of a recommendation the Minister did not agree with!

Nevertheless, I recreated the paper and sent it to Dr Goh, who wrote to the Minister for Finance, who was chairing the committee that was to approve the recommendation. In the note to the Minister, Dr Goh explained why he was recommending Truck Model B for the committee's approval even though the technical staff I headed were recommending Truck Model A.

I learnt an unforgettable lesson about leadership from this episode. The job of staff is to analyse and come up with the best answer within the bounds of their knowledge and experience. A leader is never to tell the staff to re-do their analysis, even if they should disagree with their staff's analysis for whatever reason, as they would thereby be undermining their staff's work, their sense of self-worth, and the values of honesty and integrity by telling them to write what they do not believe in.

Worst of all, they would be developing staff who do not think independently, but are instead always second-guessing their bosses. This is how organisations lose imagination, initiative, and innovative staff by ignoring their brains and undermining their courage.

Dr Goh was very generous about allowing people to learn from their mistakes. As Director of Finance, I was given the latitude to bring the management of Mindef's "block budget" to a fine art through learning by doing.

Balancing multi-year payments for major weapon systems with on-going demands to keep up the operational capability of the SAF was no straightforward task; it induced tight internal discipline and stringent oversight of expenditures. Dr Goh asked Mindef to mount an "economy drive" to assure the Ministry of Finance that Mindef was neither extravagant nor profligate in its spending.

One experiment we did was to move individual SAF units to "block

Foster Initiative and Innovation by:

- **Empowering and trusting your staff**
- **Demanding results to discover the limits of possibilities**
- **Never punishing those who find the demands too much**

Be practical about your expectations.

budgets" also. Up till then, SAF units were given standardised provisions based on predetermined rates of daily food per soldier, cleaning equipment for each camp, typewriters for each office, and so on. We looked at the operating costs for all SAF units, worked out the appropriate provisioning ratios, determined the average actual usage ratios, worked out the sums for each unit, cut the total by 15 percent, and gave the amount to the units on a "block budget" basis. The commanders were happy with the flexibilities they now had, and SAF units started studying usage and expenditure statistics they had but had never paid attention to.

It was a surprisingly happy win-win situation and many synergies were engendered. Spurred by our success, we decided to raise the cut to 25 percent from the initial 15 percent. This time, however, there were howls of pain from the ground commanders! We discovered that we had exceeded the practical limit; the rate was finally settled at around 20 percent.

I learnt much from Dr Goh about creating an organisation that fosters initiative and innovation by empowering and trusting your staff, and demanding results to discover the limits of possibilities, but never punishing those who find the demands too much.

I also learnt from Dr Goh to be practical about one's expectations. Dr Goh once decided that SAF camps should plant papaya trees to enhance the use of the land and provide an additional source of nutrition for the troops. As with any initiative, Key Performance Indictors (KPIs) were established — the number of trees, number of papayas, and so on. Not all camps were successful despite their best efforts because some terrains simply would not yield healthy papaya trees. However, rather than declare their failure, a few units took to buying papayas and papaya trees to keep up with their regular reports of the KPIs. The experiment was finally abandoned when it was plain that some units had perpetually young papaya trees! The experiment also illustrated how the disciplines of honesty and integrity can so easily be undermined when people fear to tell the truth and, in the process, the opportunity to learn and to correct poor ideas in good time was missed.

In the middle of 1978, I was assigned to be the first Principal Private Secretary to then Prime Minister Lee Kuan Yew. In 1981, I returned to Mindef as its Permanent Secretary, under a new minister, Mr Howe Yoon Chong, where I stayed until 1994.

Lift people's self-image and sense of pride.

IMAGE PROMOTION OF THE SAF

The first thing that struck me upon my return to Mindef was the low morale in the SAF. It was obvious that something had to be done to lift the self-image and sense of pride of the soldiers, as the fighting capability of any army lies not just in its equipment but fundamentally in the spirit of the soldiers — their sense of mission, the courage they bring to bear, as well as the respect and appreciation society offers them.

For too long, society had been allowed to persist with the idea that many people became soldiers because they could not find good civilian jobs. Mindef broke new ground by becoming the first government agency to mount a media campaign for image promotion; the people of the SAF were featured as "defenders of the nation," an honourable endeavour only those good enough could be trusted to take on.

Building up the public image of the SAF took on a much broader dimension than just the media campaign. An illustration is how the military rifle drill was introduced in Singapore: A national charity concert was to be held at the steps of City Hall at the Padang, and I asked the Director of SAF's internal entertainment unit, the Music and Drama Company, whether there was something we could do to put across a more military image than just have another song and dance item. The Director thought about it and suggested we do the rifle drill that he had seen in Taiwan. I concurred, and the SAF quickly got going on it. When Singaporeans saw the rifle drill on television for the first time on the night of the concert, it was a big hit, impossible without the discipline and the precision of the SAF soldiers.

TOTAL DEFENCE

This process of image building was undertaken as part of a larger message that everyone has a part to play in the defence of Singapore. Mindef launched the concept of Total Defence, an idea adapted from Switzerland and Sweden.

There are five components to Total Defence:

- Military Defence

The assurance of independence and sovereignty for Singapore lies in the spirit of Singaporeans: tough minds and warm hearts with a commitment to keep Singapore free for Singaporeans to make their own future.

- Civil Defence
- Economic Defence
- Social Defence
- Psychological Defence

Military Defence was clearly the province of the SAF. Civil Defence began within Mindef and was later transferred and built up in the Ministry of Home Affairs as the Singapore Civil Defence Force. Economic Defence was the drive for strong economic foundations for Singapore, spearheaded by all the various economic agencies such as the Monetary Authority of Singapore and the Economic Development Board. Social Defence was to ensure that racial and religious harmony is never compromised, and Singaporeans will help and look out for each other at the community level. Psychological Defence posits that the assurance of independence and sovereignty for Singapore lies in the spirit of Singaporeans: tough minds and warm hearts with a commitment to keep Singapore free for Singaporeans to make their own future.

Psychological Defence is best understood by way of what has been termed the "National Education Messages," promoted and propagated in schools and the SAF. There are six National Education Messages:

- Singapore is our homeland; this is where we belong.
- We must preserve racial and religious harmony.
- We must uphold meritocracy and incorruptibility.
- No one owes Singapore a living.
- We must ourselves defend Singapore.
- We have confidence in our future.

MINDEF PRODUCTIVITY MOVEMENT

I became Permanent Secretary in Mindef at the time when the National Productivity Movement was just starting out to promote productivity thinking and practices throughout the economy.

Intense studies were being made, especially of practices in Japanese companies on continuous improvement. Integral to the Japanese practice was the idea of workers at the shop floor being encouraged and enabled

Cultivate a spirit of enquiry, thinking, and initiative in the workplace.

to effect improvements, whether big or small, at their level; it was a mass movement urging and allowing everyone to pursue excellence.

I spoke to the chief of the SAF, asking if there was something in all this for the military. We concluded that the spirit of enquiry, thinking, and initiative at the soldier level should indeed be seen as a critical part of SAF operational capability. If our troops were on patrol in the jungle, the moment the first man turns a corner, he is on his own; we need soldiers who can think for themselves and act with courage and resourcefulness.

In an organisation like the SAF, which is intrinsically hierarchical with a tight command structure, it becomes even more critical that independent thinking and initiative be deliberately induced and promoted. The Mindef Productivity Movement comprising various components was thus born, led by the top leadership of Mindef and the SAF.

Integral to the Mindef Productivity Movement was a suggestions scheme that encouraged individuals or teams to submit suggestions on how to improve anything being done in Mindef and the SAF. Awards are given in appreciation and recognition of suggestions received, whether big or small.

Another scheme implemented to encourage thinking, questioning, initiative, and innovation was the Work Improvement Team Scheme (WITs), the Singapore Public Service's equivalent of the Quality Circles found extensively in Japanese companies, which encourage individuals to come together in teams to solve problems in their work environment. While the suggestions scheme asked participants to submit their solutions to opportunities they see for improvement, WITs asked participants to identify problems for which the solutions are not obvious and have to be methodically derived to achieve fundamental improvements. There were other elements in the Mindef Productivity Movement, such as soldier welfare and leadership development, to address productivity improvement in a holistic fashion.

CURRENTLY ESTIMATED POTENTIAL (CEP) SYSTEM

On developing the senior leadership of the SAF, then Prime Minister Lee Kuan Yew had come across a practice in Shell International for identifying their possible future top leaders through a deliberate system of assessing

Cultivate Potential.

For promotions, the rule to preserve and underline merit is clear and cannot be compromised.

No one should get promoted simply on the basis of his potential, and all promotions should be justified on the basis of performance.

the potential of their staff. A group of permanent secretaries were sent to London to study Shell's "Currently Estimated Potential (CEP) System" — the word "currently" underscoring the fact that any assessment of potential is only the best current estimate, and it could go up or down in subsequent years based on observed behaviours.

Shell's CEP system then assessed four attributes on the basis that these gave good indication of future potential, namely, Power of Analysis, Imagination, Sense of Reality, and something called Helicopter Quality, which is the ability to see things in their broad context but at the same time having the ability to focus on critical details (much like how a helicopter can offer a panoramic view at high altitude but can also come down to low levels to attend to details).

I found the CEP concept extremely interesting and decided we should try it out, suitably modified, in Mindef. A system was thus introduced in Mindef where every officer is assessed for performance and for potential every year. Nevertheless, the rule to preserve and underline merit is clear and cannot be compromised: no one gets promoted on the basis of his potential, and all promotions have to be justified on the basis of performance. Hence, a staff with high potential but who does not exercise his potential through performance will not be promoted, while a person with higher potential backed up by superior performance can be promoted faster than a person with lower potential.

In addition, to cater for the specific needs of the SAF, every officer had a "Command CEP" that assessed his capacity in a command position, and a "Staff CEP" that assessed his capacity for staff work; officers in specialist fields such as medicine or engineering could have a third CEP designated as his "Specialist CEP." It all made for a more refined system of knowing the future leadership capacity in the SAF, and a fairer and more rational system for promoting and developing the officers.

SCENARIO PLANNING

Yet another innovation learnt from Shell International that was introduced in Mindef was that of scenario planning, which helps prepare organisations for uncertain futures.

Scenario planning posits scenarios that are plausible and possible,

Prepare for Uncertain Futures.

without assigning probabilities to them. It recognises that while some elements such as population demographics can be forecast to a considerable degree of accuracy, there are critical uncertainties that could cause the world to turn out in several different ways. Organisations should always try to take advantage of the scenarios as they unfold, and at the same time be able to mitigate their ill effects. Scenario planning was thus introduced in Mindef to help the SAF work out plans and strategies to deal with different possible futures.

IN CLOSING...

My thirteen years as Permanent Secretary of Mindef were exciting, motivating, and intensely satisfying, as there was freedom for much innovation, creativity, and experimentation. Assuring the security of Singapore demanded deep thought, much imagination, and continuous learning by doing. Everything had to be done to deliver the best possible operationally capable SAF within the financial and human resources of the ministry and country. The call was for tough minds to make difficult decisions with conviction and courage, and at the same time for warm hearts to empathise with the hopes and dreams of Singaporeans for peace, security, and a worthy future for themselves and their children.

I had learnt what it took to lift the spirits of the people in Mindef, to identify and develop leadership, and to plan and prepare for uncertain futures, but I never fully understood what I had learnt until I left Mindef to head three other ministries for the next 12 years before I retired from the civil service.

CHALLENGE 4

LEARN BY DOING

When my first granddaughter was just over a year old, I saw her trying to take a small tube of toothpaste out of its box. Her little fingers did not have the strength to grip the tube to pull it out. She was very frustrated and shook the box around.

Suddenly, when the box was upside down, the toothpaste tube fell out.

Now that she had gotten it out, she decided she wanted to put it back in. So she put the box upright, and put the tube in.

Then what did she do?

She turned the box upside down and made the toothpaste tube fall out again. She then put it back into the box. Again and again, she made the tube fall out and put it back in the box.

What was happening?

She was having fun learning a new way to take something out of a box! You can try to pull it out. You can also turn the box upside down to make it fall out.

But I was learning something important also ...

We can learn by copying what others do. It is a good way of learning. But it also means we will always be behind them.

If we want to be ahead, we must also learn by trying new ways, by experimenting, by "shaking things about" and watching what happens.

The point is to Learn by Doing. Don't just talk. Don't just think. Do!

Confucius, the great Chinese teacher and thinker who lived from 551BC to 479BC, taught something important about learning by doing. He said:

"I hear and I forget.
I see and I remember.
I do and I understand."

Do you find this to be true in your life? It is only when you *do* something that you really understand what you actually have to do, how to do it, and why you are doing it.

Don't just take note of them. Think about how to put the Public Service values of Integrity, Service, and Excellence into action. Make them real. Make them part of your life. Try and try again. Do and do again. Not just the same old ways but also in new ways.

Learn by Doing.

CHAPTER 4

Nothing in our past is wasted.

Everything can be built upon to help us make the future.

Chapter 4

SYSTEMS FOR SUCCESS

Throughout all the opportunities I was given to contribute to the advancement of the civil service and Singapore, I have discovered that people want to do good work and succeed, and that the ultimate expression of appreciation and recognition we can give them lies in allowing them to contribute what they can towards the progress and improvement of their organisation and their work.

Remarkably, I found my years of experience and experimentation in Mindef were not only relevant for my work post-Mindef, but also the very reason why I could advocate and lead change with confidence and understanding in the places I went to after Mindef. Nothing in our past is wasted; everything can be built upon to help us make the future.

Building upon my experience at Mindef, I had the wonderful opportunity to launch a mass movement for the pursuit of excellence in the civil service in 1995, called "PS21," an acronym for "Public Service for the 21st Century," which I will go into further detail in the next chapter.

1994–1998: PUBLIC SERVICE DIVISION (PSD) OF THE PRIME MINISTER'S OFFICE

I was with the Public Service Division (PSD) of the Prime Minister's Office from 1994 to 1998. PSD was the Division in charge of personnel policy for the civil service, but I was convinced it should do a lot more than just human resource functions; it should also address the issue of what all the personnel in the civil service are for and how they deliver service to their customers (the Singapore public and businesses) in a way that

The civil service should not only meet the needs of today; it should also anticipate the needs for tomorrow.

The Currently Estimated Potential (CEP) System goes beyond the whats and hows of what an employee does, to focus on the whys and why nots that drive the way he or she analyses issues, imagines solutions, and seeks practical outcomes.

is responsive to their needs, with the quality and courtesy they deserve. Above all, the civil service would need to not only meet the needs of today, but also anticipate the needs for tomorrow.

The Singapore Civil Service was already widely acknowledged internationally as an exemplary service, but I believed it could be the best civil service in the world, on a sustained and sustainable basis. I sought to achieve this vision by:

- Systematising the personnel system for assessing the potential and performance of all officers in the civil service
- Pursuing excellence in every dimension through PS21
- Introducing scenario planning into the system

The first built upon my experience with the CEP (Currently Estimated Potential) and personnel system I had developed in Mindef; the second built upon my experience in launching the Mindef Productivity Movement; and the third built upon my experience with introducing scenario planning in Mindef. These were therefore "mass launches" of what were already working in Mindef. The fact that I brought with me experience from Mindef facilitated in a major way the acceptance of — or at least the willingness to try — the changes for the civil service.

CURRENTLY ESTIMATED POTENTIAL (CEP) SYSTEM

The CEP system was already in place in parts of the civil service when I joined the Public Service Division in 1994. I believed that if what we wanted was to help people be the best they can be, we must go beyond looking just at performance to also deliberately assess the potential of every staff. The CEP system goes beyond the whats and hows of what an employee does, to focus on the whys and why nots that drive the way he or she analyses issues, imagines solutions, and seeks practical outcomes.

In order to mitigate individual biases, I introduced a disciplined and systematic way, based on ranking by panels, to assess the performance and potential of every officer, and make the subsequent decisions on promotions, increments, and bonuses. While it was clear that no one could ever claim that there was no subjectivity in the system, given that

PUBLIC SERVICE FOR THE 21ST CENTURY (PS21) addresses:

- How to make change a welcome part of work
- How to anticipate change as best as possible
- How to execute change with maximum effectiveness and efficiency

To meet demands for service, performance, economy, and timeliness in delivery, leaders must first pay attention to their staff's well-being — not just their physical needs, but also their social, mental, and emotional well-being.

Scenario planning was introduced into the civil service to establish a "dialogue" with the political leadership for the purposes of long-term planning for Singapore.

the very process of judging individuals is subjective and there will always be those who feel that they have not been assessed fairly, the real practical question at hand was whether the civil service and individuals as a whole were better off with, or without, the system.

PUBLIC SERVICE FOR THE 21ST CENTURY (PS21)

PS21 was introduced so that public officers in government service may contribute as best they can to make their organisation the best it can be, thereby enabling the organisation to go beyond today's performance to attain tomorrow's potential. PS21 tries to do for the organisation through its people, what the CEP based system tries to do for the individual; it addresses how to make change a welcome part of work, how to anticipate change as best as possible, and how to execute change with maximum effectiveness and efficiency.

PS21 also recognises that individuals are subject to customer demand for service and performance, and at the same time their supervisors' demands for economy and timeliness in outputs and outcomes. To meet these demands, staff need to be well-trained, allowed to exercise initiative and imagination, and continuously learn from experience, trials, and mistakes; for all these, the starting point must be attention to their well-being, not just their physical needs, but also their social, mental, and emotional well-being, because no one can be expected to give of his or her best if they do not believe the organisation cares for them.

SCENARIO PLANNING

Scenario planning was introduced into the civil service to establish a "dialogue" with the political leadership for the purposes of long-term planning for Singapore. While the elected government could feel reasonably confident about planning for the next year or even next three to five years, the fact is that no one can sensibly be confident about looking ahead for the next 10, 20 or 30 years. However, a country critically needs longer term planning to establish firm foundations for new possibilities in the coming years.

Let us take education as an example. The process starts even before a

A country critically needs longer term planning to establish firm foundations for new possibilities in the coming years.

Scenario planning is even more critical for Singapore due to its smallness and lack of natural resources.

kid gets to school: The period from school entry to leaving for university is 12 years, so whoever plans education should have some sense about needs more than 10 years into the future. Similarly with other aspects of government such as defence, housing, healthcare, urban planning, land reclamation, water supply, and so on.

Scenario planning is even more critical for Singapore due to its smallness and lack of natural resources; its survival and success is based on alertness, agility, pragmatism, creativity, tough-mindedness, courage, leadership, and enterprise.

I envisaged scenario planning as the way to strike an understanding between the civil service leadership and the political leadership as to what the future environment could be like and how Singapore should position itself for these different futures.

The first set of national scenarios had two scenarios dealing with the external geopolitical and economic environment, and two scenarios dealing with the domestic environment titled "Hotel Singapore" and "Home Divided."

"Hotel Singapore" posited the possibility of Singaporeans leaving Singapore if the situation became challenging and uncomfortable, rather than staying to confront the obstacles and work out solutions, while "Home Divided" posited the possibility of Singaporean society being fragmented by divides based on race, religion, incomes, and so on.

It is very important never to forget that scenarios are not predictions and their usefulness for planning lies in envisaging futures that may not be pleasant, but are nonetheless possible. From these, appropriate strategies are developed and executed to mitigate the negative consequences that may arise from neglect and also to seize the opportunities that the scenarios bring to the fore. The idea is to help prepare and equip Singaporeans in good time with the appropriate knowledge and skills, backed up by fortitude and determination.

1997–1999: MINISTRY OF EDUCATION

When I moved on to the Ministry of Education in 1997, I found a highly motivated people who believed in the worthiness of their cause and had

The three phases of development of the Singapore education system can be summarised as:

- Survival-driven
- Efficiency-driven
- Ability-driven

a burning desire to do a great job in moulding the future of the nation that passed through their hands; but I also found an education system that was due for a thorough review.

I gathered 320 teachers from across the school education system to address 32 different topics that the senior leadership had identified as ripe for review. The 320 teachers in turn involved large numbers of other teachers as they sought to understand the issues and develop ideas for improvement or initiation.

The result of the review was succinctly summarised as a process of moving the education system through three phases from the time of Singapore's internal self-government.

The three phases of development of the Singapore education system can be summarised as:

- Survival-driven (1959-78)
- Efficiency-driven (1979-96)
- Ability-driven (post 1997)

Survival-driven Phase: The Survival-driven phase started in 1959 and took on an urgent salience when Singapore suddenly became independent in 1965; the focus in this 19-year phase was on generating school places for every child, at least in primary school. Schools were built at a tremendous pace and the number of teachers almost doubled, but "wastage" was high, with no better illustration than the need for Mindef to set up "Hokkien platoons" in the SAF units where the language of instruction was neither English nor Mandarin but Hokkien, the Chinese dialect most widely spoken in Singapore, to cater for the full-time national servicemen who had left school literate in neither English nor Mandarin.

Efficiency-driven Phase: The Efficiency-driven phase commenced in 1979 and lasted about 17 years. It was characterised by: (1) centrally produced teaching materials to enable the many less-experienced teachers to deliver good lessons, and (2) widespread streaming of students according to their academic ability, as teachers would find it more practical to handle the relatively large classes if they comprised students of similar ability. As the teacher population grew in numbers and self-confidence, greater

The next phase of the education system should be more driven by values with a heavier emphasis on:

- **Thought**
- **Enterprise**
- **Self-confidence**

flexibility and autonomy were given to an increasing number of schools to cater to the capabilities of their particular cohorts of students. This was formalised after the extensive reviews of 1997.

Ability-driven Phase: The Ability-driven phase that started in 1997 was focussed on helping each child attain his or her potential, whether it be in the academic or non-academic spheres. It was launched with the "Thinking Schools, Learning Nation" movement, where schools became more peer-driven in self-developed targets of achievement, and the ministry headquarters moved to see its role much more as encouraging, supporting, and enhancing school achievement rather than directing them.

The Ability-driven phase is now more than 15 years old, about the time it takes a child to go from Primary One to graduate from university, and it is time for a review. I posit that the next phase should be more driven by values with a heavier emphasis on thought, enterprise, and self-confidence.

There was a ferment of ideas and possibilities in the short two years I was with the Ministry of Education. I heard many calls to focus on just a few ideas rather than have so many changes being put out at the same time.

My view, however, was that the education system was uniquely one where curriculums were developed by specialists at the centre; while each specialist judges his or her success according to how well the curriculum proposals get adopted and executed in the schools, each school has to be able to decide what to implement, to what extent, and at what rate according to what it assesses would be most relevant for its cohort of students whose backgrounds, abilities, and interests vary within each school and, even more, between schools.

My belief was that the principals of schools should be given the prerogative to decide what and how their respective schools are to take on these new proposals from the headquarters of the Ministry of Education according to their knowledge of their own students. Hence, the centre should not be restricted on the number of new proposals they could put out, but the prerogative should be left to the principals to decide what to take up and adopt.

I look upon my time in the Ministry of Education with enormous

There is something very special about being a teacher.

The teacher has to deal with the largely indefinable outcome called "helping every child realise his or her potential," and the ultimate test has to be whether each child actually realises his or her potential to the fullest.

Because of this very special characteristic of teaching, the morale, dedication, and motivation of teachers are paramount if the best student outcomes are to be achieved.

Building up the standing of teachers and giving every support to teachers to get their task done well is the key to running a superior education system.

satisfaction. The morale of teachers and principals was lifted, and the focus was put exactly where it should be in any education system: the students, whose futures are being moulded through developing their self-confidence according to their respective capabilities, their ability to think for themselves, their desire to be continuously learning in life, and their understanding that the greatest satisfaction in life lies not simply in getting and receiving, but in giving and contributing.

There is something very special about being a teacher that makes the profession distinctly different from any other. In the office, for example, each one plays his or her role to serve the boss in meeting his vision and the mission of the company or organisation. If the staff fails to perform his or her role, the boss suffers, so if there should be any lapse, the boss has every incentive to help the staff succeed or to remove him or her.

If the vision of the boss is defective, the organisation fails to fulfil its mission and it will be only a matter of time before the boss is removed. So the boss has every reason to make sure his vision is congruent with the mission of the organisation, and to make sure his staff do all they can to align with the vision.

All these are different in teaching in a very critical way. The teacher has to deal with the largely indefinable outcome called "helping every child realise his or her potential." Who defines the potential? Who identifies the potential? Who strives to help the child realise the potential? It is the child's teachers, so everything depends on the teachers' personal commitment and dedication to doing everything they can for the children in their care.

Yet the teacher who is defective in this but gets on well with the boss (i.e. the principal) is not likely to get into trouble with the boss, while the children may be suffering for lack of guidance or support or attention from the teacher. Principals would have their respective visions for the school, and they would expect their teachers to give full support in realising the vision, but the ultimate test has to be whether each child actually realises his or her potential to the fullest.

Because of this very special characteristic of teaching, the morale, dedication, and motivation of teachers are paramount if the best student outcomes are to be achieved. Building up the standing of teachers and giving every support to teachers to get their task done well is the key to running a superior education system. I sought to build the standing and

The concept of the Reinvestment Fund dispensed with unnecessary discussion and "story telling," and established budget staff as active players in developing Singapore for the future by allocating funds for the best new ideas.

self-perception of teachers, just as I did what I could to build the morale and self-pride of soldiers in the SAF.

1998–2006: MINISTRY OF FINANCE (MOF)

When I started my appointment at the MOF in 1998, I found that, not unlike other countries, officers in the MOF saw themselves as controllers of the budget; thus, they oftentimes started on the assumption that government agencies will always ask for too much, and therefore, they would have done their job well when they cut back on budget requests.

While some officers may have found pleasure and purpose in cutting down on others' requests, I felt the task less than motivating and worth doing. Government agencies had over the years learnt to over-request so that the budget officers in the MOF could have the pleasure of cutting down the budget requests; this way both sides end up being happy. Budget sessions had become good "story telling" sessions by the various ministries and government agencies to convince the MOF the worthiness of their proposals.

I decided to change the *modus operandi*. Using my experience in Mindef with "block budgets," I decided it would be a good idea to pre-specify "block budgets" in every ministry in order to achieve "more for the dollar" by pre-determining their expenditure budget, maximising their scope for discretion, measuring their costs, and encouraging them to pursue excellence.

To start with, we took the average of what each ministry had spent in recent years as a percentage of the Gross Domestic Product (GDP), raised the sum by the anticipated GDP growth for the next financial year, and cut back the sum by a presumed "productivity dividend." The ministries were then told what their "block budgets" would be, for which they had to tell the MOF what indicators they were going to use to assure good use of the funds. All the collections from the "productivity dividends" were then put into a "central pot" called the Reinvestment Fund; ministries desiring additional funds for new proposals were then invited to submit their requests for allocations from the Reinvestment Fund.

This way the ideas across government had to compete against each other for funding, while funds for day-to-day operations were allocated

MOF introduced the "balanced scorecard" so that outcomes, not budgets, were the drivers of behaviour.

THE MOF WAY:

- **M**otivate staff to take pride in service-enhancing initiative and creativity

- **O**vercome obstacles in systems and policies to achieve superior results that are sustainable

- **F**ocus on excellence through innovation and quality in customer service

without argument. Not only was unnecessary discussion and "story telling" dispensed with, the budget staff of the MOF were also now no longer "policemen" trying to catch ministries off-guard, but instead were active players in developing Singapore for the future by allocating funds for the best new ideas. The sense of purpose was raised and morale went up. Everyone was focussed on their dreams for the Singapore they wished to see.

Another innovation introduced by the MOF was the "balanced scorecard" that companies in the private sector were using not just to drive their on-going financial performance, but also to measure the sustainability of that performance by investing in people and processes. The "balanced scorecard" required ministries to define and monitor the most critical outcomes they sought, measured the financial resources they used in the process, checked on their processes to drive for efficiency and effectiveness, and monitored the training and development of their staff to assure sustainability of performance. Budgets were not the drivers of behaviour; outcomes were the drivers of behaviour, with budgets as the necessary support.

To provide the compass for the MOF's strategic evolution, I introduced THE MOF WAY, which outlined how to pursue and sustain excellence through leadership and system management within a culture of integrity and openness. The framework was supported by the ministry's core values: Integrity, Caring, Innovative, Team, and Excellence or I-CITE (pronounced "eyesight"). Three ideas drove the behaviour of the MOF team:

- **M**otivate staff to take pride in service-enhancing initiative and creativity
- **O**vercome obstacles in systems and policies to achieve superior results that are sustainable
- **F**ocus on excellence through innovation and quality in customer service

THE MOF Way set People as the originator of all achievement; Systems for efficiency, consistency, and sustainability; and Citizens and Customers as the reason for everything the MOF did. It was people centred, systems oriented, as well as citizen and customer focussed.

The rule that the top two appointments of Permanent Secretary and Deputy Secretary in the various ministries are to retire after 10 years in the job grade assured a continuing flow of talent, as well as a disciplined, organised, and systematic regeneration of top civil service leadership.

AFTER THE CIVIL SERVICE (2006–PRESENT)

When I retired from the civil service in 2006, I was approached to chair the Economic Development Board. I retired at the age of 59 years, which was earlier than the national retirement age of 62, following a rule I had advocated when I was the Head of Civil Service, where officers in the top two appointments of Permanent Secretary and Deputy Secretary in the various ministries are to retire after 10 years in the job grade.

I had implemented this rule to assure a continuing flow of talent, as I believed that the regeneration of top civil service leadership had to be a disciplined, organised, and systematic process. If there were no regular retirement of officers at the topmost jobs, younger officers were likely to decide to leave the civil service at an early age. This would have serious impact on the capability of government over the long term, as the complexity of government was such that the grooming process for top leadership required officers to be rotated around various functions of government for exposure, for learning, and for building a network of contacts.

I had imagined that on retirement I would be enjoying my grand-children and experimenting with their development and growth in ways I had not done or could not do with my own children. Thus, when I was approached to chair the Singapore Economic Development Board (EDB), I was somewhat reluctant to take on the appointment. However, being a Christian, I decided to submit the matter to God in prayer. God reminded me that I had moved from position to position in the civil service without my ever asking for a next appointment or promotion; it was all God's providence, and this was His next step for my life. I thus agreed to take on the appointment at EDB.

The mission of the EDB is to attract, promote, and support direct investments that would give Singapore an economic edge and create the economic future for Singapore; hence, my appointment as the Chairman of EDB gave me a new sphere of experience in having to "market" Singapore as a regional, if not global, hub for business activities.

The orientation of EDB was perpetually the future, and thus I found myself serving yet another future-oriented enterprise like I had enjoyed in the Ministry of Defence, the Prime Minister's Office, the Ministry of

If we get the thinking and practice right, we will be on a good track to the future; but if we get them wrong, we will reap tepid performance, low morale, dysfunctional relations, and a tragic waste of human capability and organisational potential.

Education, and the Ministry of Finance. I have always found it energising to be engaged in "creating the future" through having people offer their best because the work is interesting, challenging, purposeful, and worthwhile. When people are fully engaged with their hearts and minds, they grow in self-confidence as they make possible what others dismiss as impossible.

Just one year later I was asked to take on the position of Group President of GIC Private Limited, the government's fund manager for Singapore's foreign reserves. Again I demurred and turned down the approach twice as it was not my idea of retirement, but again God reminded me to trust Him, so I agreed the third time I was asked.

I held the two portfolios at EDB and GIC concurrently for two years, before I finally went full-time with GIC in 2009. I believe that God has His ways and His purposes, which we can quickly understand in some cases, yet in other cases, might never understand in this life on Earth.

IN CLOSING...

I have had a very good run of opportunities to make a difference in every place I have been. What has been most important to me has been the privilege of offering people purpose in their work, and providing them with opportunities to stretch themselves to the maximum and make their contribution to a worthy future.

In the next chapter, I discuss governance and PS21, which is the civil service movement in the pursuit of excellence, following which I discuss the culture and values required to bring organisations to achieve superior performance on a sustainable and sustained basis.

If we get the thinking and practice right, we will be on a good track to the future; but if we get them wrong, we will reap tepid performance, low morale, dysfunctional relations, and a tragic waste of human capability and organisational potential.

CHALLENGE 5

THINK... AND THINK AGAIN

About 20 years ago, I spoke to a Singaporean who had studied in Japan. He was working for a Japanese company in Singapore. It was the start of the National Productivity Movement, and Singapore wanted to learn as much as possible from the Japanese about productivity.

I asked him, "What is the difference between the Japanese and the Singaporean? How is it that Japanese companies can get all their people to keep thinking up new ways to improve their work? How is it they can keep coming up with new designs for the many things the Japanese make so well, such as cars and cameras?"

He said, "It all starts from young. The Japanese are taught from young to think about what they are doing and to know why they are doing it. That is why Japanese workers keep thinking about better ways for doing things and better things to do."

"Think of a Japanese father who is trying to hang a picture. He asks his son to bring him a nail. If the son simply brings him a nail, he will ask, 'Where is the hammer?' The son will say 'I am sorry I did not bring the hammer.' He goes to get the hammer."

"Now imagine a Singaporean father trying to hang a picture.

He asks his son to bring him a nail. If the son simply brings him a nail, and he asks, 'Where is the hammer?' What do you think the son will say? Will he say 'sorry'? Or will he say, 'You did not ask me to bring a hammer.'"

We should not simply do what we are asked to do. We should always ask, "What am I doing this for?" Then think of what else we should do. Think of a better way to do it. Think also of completely different things to do that are useful, sensible, and effective. That is how we become better and better.

Let us remember: Don't just get the nail. Where is the hammer? Should we hang the picture on a different wall? Should we hang a different picture? Should we get a sculpture instead? Is the purpose to hang the picture? Or is the purpose to make the room look better?

Think ... and think again.

CHAPTER 5

"Setting the rule is the government's business, to give maximum freedom to the individual without impinging unreasonably on the freedom of others; converting the heart is God's business."

Dr Goh Keng Swee

Chapter 5

GOVERNANCE AND PUBLIC SERVICE FOR THE 21ST CENTURY

We have a rule in Singapore that if you are having a loud party and your neighbour complains, the police will ask you to stop the noise if it is after midnight so that the neighbours may have their quiet and get to sleep.

I remember very well a conversation I had with Dr Goh Keng Swee over this rule. Dr Goh said it was a rule that tried to be fair: People can have a good time and enjoy themselves with loud laughter, singing, and music, but only till midnight; the neighbours must be allowed to have quiet for their sleep after midnight.

I asked if it would not be better for people to be educated about social responsibility and how to care for their neighbours; then they will naturally stop making so much noise that it upsets their neighbours, and perhaps they may even stop the music before midnight.

Dr Goh, in his usual practical and incisive wisdom, said, "Setting the rule is the government's business, to give maximum freedom to the individual without impinging unreasonably on the freedom of others; converting the heart is God's business." What a marvellous explanation of what is the role of the government and what are the forces beyond the realm of government!

ROLE OF THE GOVERNMENT

What is the role of the government?

It is generally expected that the government is to provide safety and security, law and order, accountability, economic development, social justice, citizen participation, as well as efficiency and effectiveness in the

The government serves as:

- **Controller and Regulator**
- **Nurturer and Facilitator**
- **Convenor and Aggregator**

Governments tend to be uncomfortable with the last role — convenor and aggregator — because the outcomes are not predictable and the government can easily find itself in a dilemma of showing it is prepared to listen and gather ideas, and yet is unprepared to actually act upon them.

Changing demographics suggest that governments that do not become more active in the third role, while maintaining high performance in the first and second roles, run the danger of losing citizen support.

delivery of government services by governing with a judicious mix of functions and involvement of the public sector, the private sector, and the people sector (also referred to in other countries as "the third sector").

The government can be said traditionally to perform the role of controller and regulator: controlling the national assets and regulating the functioning of society and the economy to deliver safety, security, law, and order to the citizenry. This is fundamentally the responsibility of the public sector.

An extension of the government's role is that of nurturer and facilitator by encouraging, seeding, promoting, developing or allowing activities that enhance daily life and the development of the economy and the country. This is mostly the domain of the private sector for business activities and the people sector for social services.

And finally, the role of government expands into that of convening and aggregating: convening or getting people together, either physically or virtually, to put forth ideas, advocate, discuss, and argue the merits of different proposals, and aggregating the best proposals into some framework which the government can support and promote with talent and resources. This is very much the sphere of the people sector — citizen involvement in shaping the development and functioning of the country, yet requiring government support to advance the agenda.

Governments tend to be very comfortable with the first two roles — controller and regulator, and nurturer and facilitator — because the actions, and therefore also the outcomes, tend to be easier for the government to manage.

Governments, however, also tend to be uncomfortable with the last role — convenor and aggregator — because the outcomes are not predictable and the government can easily find itself in a dilemma of showing it is prepared to listen and gather ideas, and yet is unprepared to actually act upon them. Yet the changing demographics in terms of age profiles, education level, socioeconomic improvements, a desire to be involved and have a say, as well as wide exposure to the media and the world, suggest that governments that do not become more active in the third role, while maintaining high performance in the first and second roles, run the danger of losing citizen support.

Perhaps uniquely among countries, the Singapore government has

Four principles of governance:

- **Leadership is Key**
- **Anticipate Change; Stay Relevant**
- **Reward for Work; Work for Reward**
- **A Stake for Everyone; Opportunities for All**

The political leadership decides policy, while the civil service has to deliver the policy the best way possible.

The civil service is impartial but not neutral.

When delivering its service, the civil service has to be impartial with respect to race, religion, socioeconomic status, and so on; but the civil service cannot be neutral with respect to executing the policy.

explicitly stated a set of principles of governance that Prime Minister Lee Hsien Loong spoke of on 23 October 2004. These four principles have undergirded the governance of Singapore since internal self-government in 1959 through independence in 1965, up to the present:

- **Leadership is Key**: Leaders must have vision with moral courage and integrity, and conviction to do what is right and not necessarily what is popular.

- **Anticipate Change; Stay Relevant**: Be open to new ideas, keep questioning old assumptions, and never be trapped in the past.

- **Reward for Work; Work for Reward**: No one owes the country a living. Be self-reliant and strike a good balance between individual responsibility and an appropriate safety net.

- **A Stake for Everyone; Opportunities for All**: Create an inclusive society in which citizens feel a sense of ownership and belonging.

ROLES OF POLITICAL LEADERSHIP AND THE CIVIL SERVICE

The question has often been asked, "What are the respective roles of the political leadership and the civil service?"

The political leadership decides policy, while the civil service has to deliver the policy the best way possible. While the civil service helps in the development of the policy, its primary input must be with an eye on how well the policy can be executed and how sustainable it is.

Defining the policy outcomes has to be a political prerogative and responsibility. It is for the political leadership to assess what policy outcomes would serve the needs and aspirations of the citizens best; it is not for the civil service to decide between the many different ideas and desires of the electorate.

This principle is expressed succinctly in the statement: The civil service is impartial but not neutral. In other words, when delivering its service, the civil service has to be impartial with respect to race, religion, socioeconomic status, and so on; but the civil service cannot be neutral with respect to executing the policy as the civil service is the government's instrument for public policy.

The civil service needs to be responsive to two developments:

- A public that is increasingly vocal and demanding of higher standards of service
- An economy that has to operate within an increasingly interconnected world

The public service must learn to anticipate demands and meet needs in ways that are innovative, and create conditions for the country to stay ahead tomorrow.

PS21 is basically a challenge about change: not a change to a specific final state but an acceptance of the need for change as a permanent state.

The primary role of the civil service is delivery, and the challenge the civil service has to meet is to perform its role efficiently and effectively, as well as responsively and responsibly, with due regard to quality and courtesy.

FUNDAMENTALS OF GOOD GOVERNANCE

The fundamentals of good governance are a clean and effective government that is corruption-free, meritocratic, efficient, responsive, fair, and impartial. But current success is no guarantee of future success, especially when that future may bear little resemblance to the present. Failure to change in good time is often the failure to change in good times.

The question is whether these fundamentals of governance are good enough for the future: a future of greater complexity, exploding information flow, much less predictability, and shorter reaction times.

In particular, the civil service needs to be responsive to two developments: a public that is increasingly vocal and demanding of higher standards of service, and an economy that has to operate within an increasingly interconnected world.

The public service must learn to anticipate demands and meet needs in ways that are innovative. The capacity to create conditions for the country to stay ahead in the competition of tomorrow must expand. To this end, the Singapore civil service mounted a public–sector-wide initiative in a drive for organisational excellence. Its purpose was to position the public service for superior capability and delivery in the 21st century.

"PUBLIC SERVICE FOR THE 21ST CENTURY" ("PS21")

"Public Service for the 21st Century" or "PS21" was launched in May 1995. PS21 is basically a challenge about change: not a change to a specific final state but an acceptance of the need for change as a permanent state.

It is not difficult for many public officers to see their job principally as that of observing rules and following precedents; while the rules have generally proven useful, and the precedents are part of a successful

PS21 had two objectives:

- To nurture an attitude of service excellence in meeting the needs of the public with high standards of quality and courtesy
- To foster an environment that induces and welcomes continuous change for greater efficiency and cost-effectiveness by employing modern management tools and techniques, while paying attention to the morale and welfare of public officers

Welcoming change is opening the mental window to see change as an opportunity rather than a threat.

past, they do not guarantee a successful future. Thus, the qualities of consistency and continuity, perceived as the virtues of public service, will prove to be limitations unless the qualities of flexibility and enterprise are incorporated into the system.

OBJECTIVES OF PS21

PS21 had two objectives:

- To nurture an attitude of service excellence in meeting the needs of the public with high standards of quality and courtesy
- To foster an environment that induces and welcomes continuous change for greater efficiency and cost-effectiveness by employing modern management tools and techniques, while paying attention to the morale and welfare of public officers

In many ways, the second objective encompasses the first. The first was included to induce a certain tangibility to how people are to think of PS21. The second is much more fundamental: it involves transforming mind-sets and creating a different organisational culture and norms; this different mind-set about change involves welcoming change, anticipating change, and executing change.

Welcoming change is opening the mental window to see change as an opportunity rather than a threat. PS21 adopted the approach of making everyone an activist for change and improvement. PS21 also used scenario-based planning to anticipate change and prepare for alternative landscapes. Finally, the execution of change was achieved through the superior management of people and resources.

FOCUS AREAS OF PS21

To bring about this mind-set change in the public service, PS21 focussed on four areas:

- Staff Well-Being
- Excellence through Continuous Enterprise and Learning (ExCEL)

"PS21" in a Nutshell:

THEME	Continuous Change
REASON	Unending Uncertainty
THRUST	Change as a Way of Life
MEANS	Harnessing Creativity
GOAL	Be in Time for the Future
AREAS OF FOCUS	• Staff Well-Being • Excellence through Continuous Enterprise and Learning (ExCEL) • Organisational Review • Quality Service

- Organisational Review
- Quality Service

Staff Well-Being and ExCEL are people-focussed initiatives: the former to convince them that the organisation cares about their well-being, and the latter to give them the foundation and environment to release the spirit of innovation and creativity. Organisational Review is management-driven change in systems and procedures, as well as organisational direction to bring about change. Quality Service focuses on customer-orientation in a continuous drive for service excellence.

Staff Well-Being comes first because the individual is the critical member in the whole process of change: how one sees oneself will determine whether one has the confidence and desire to contribute to change.

Excellence through Continuous Enterprise and Learning (ExCEL) is about the officer's attitude towards continuous improvement, and how one sees one's work. As public officers are used to directions coming top down, it is necessary to provide a formal framework for generating ideas from the bottom up. The Work Improvement Team Scheme (WITs) — the Public Service's version of Quality Circles — and the Staff Suggestions Scheme (SSS) — are two critical channels for this. About 90 percent of all public officers participated in the WITs movement, and overall there was more than one improvement suggestion per officer each year. Continuous learning complements the WITs and SSS imperatives of looking for continuous improvement, with a general target of every public officer having 100 hours of learning a year, which may involve formal or informal training, and any way of learning.

Organisational Review is change driven by management. While individual officers at the operating level are encouraged to actively suggest, promote, and pursue change, they are powerless to introduce multi-agency or multi-departmental change, or to deal with procedural bottlenecks involving other work units or ministries. Therefore, supervisors must take the initiative to harness information technology, reduce red tape, and pursue innovation.

To achieve Quality Service, the public service must never forget to CARE:

Courtesy: it is not only what you do, but how you do it

Accessibility: where and when you do it

Responsiveness: whether you do it in good time

Effectiveness: whether you meet the customer's needs or even exceed his expectations

Quality Service: Customers demand and deserve Quality Service. Quality is how the customer defines it, and the aim of the service provider must be to exceed the customer's expectations. In a comprehensive sense, the customer is anyone who expects a response from us, anyone we hope to get a response from, and anyone we are passing our work to next. In other words, the customer is anyone we have a connection with! Thus, a customer could be external (e.g. a member of the public or a business associate) or internal (e.g. a colleague, a supervisor, or a subordinate).

To achieve Quality Service, the public service must never forget to CARE:

Courtesy: it is not only what you do, but how you do it

Accessibility: where and when you do it

Responsiveness: whether you do it in good time

Effectiveness: whether you meet the customer's needs or even exceed his expectations

GOAL OF PS21

The goal of PS21 is the transformation of the Singapore Public Service: from reactivity to proactivity, from a satisfaction with the present to a questioning of the future. This demands a change in approach, values, and culture in various important ways.

Beyond Performance to Potential: The success of any organisation depends on how well it mobilises its resources. How can creativity be harnessed, interest maintained, performance enhanced, and output optimised?

Such success lies in giving officers the opportunity to develop their abilities, demonstrate their potential, and be the best that they can be. It also lies in putting the best person in charge, who can then create the conditions for others to contribute.

The Singapore Public Service constantly appraises officers to gauge how far they can go. Those assessed to have higher potential are given the more difficult jobs to prove their worth. Bonus awards are tied to real performance, not potential *per se*. When the person's assessed

Leaders should look:

- **Beyond Performance to Potential**
- **Beyond Results to Process**
- **Beyond Coordinated Action to Coordinated Vision**
- **Beyond Least for Output to Most for Input**
- **Beyond Management to Leadership**

Getting the underlying process right will better assure that the desired outcome may be achieved again and again in the future.

potential is confirmed by his performance on the job, he gets promoted to a higher grade.

In essence, the Service looks beyond the officer's performance to assess and develop his potential in a conscious, deliberate manner, and achieves superior organisational performance through the practice of meritocracy.

Beyond Results to Process: An organisation cannot afford to judge itself by results alone — it is not that results are unimportant, but rather that the quality of the process that brings them about is more important. Getting the results right one or two times is no guarantee that the success will repeat itself; however, getting the underlying process right will better assure that the desired outcome may be achieved again and again in the future.

The process mentioned here refers to always wanting to do things better and always questioning how to better prepare for the future. It is not simply about maintaining today's rules and regulations as this would lead to mindless execution, bureaucracy, and unresponsiveness. The PS21 movement seeks to make the Public Service a more thinking and creative organisation.

Beyond Coordinated Action to Coordinated Vision: Scenario-based planning is a most critical aspect of PS21. It helps an organisation think about a future that is uncertain and unpredictable. Through the process of scenario-based planning, everyone becomes attuned and sensitised to the signals of change, and we learn to think with a contingency mind-set so we may be able to react quickly when the need arises.

Scenario-based planning is particularly valuable for a small country such as Singapore, as she has little influence and control over what happens in the world and the region. Internally, it is often the case that the action of one ministry or government department has an impact on the work of another. Many issues span across more than one ministry. Operating in a decentralised system provides for quicker response and greater efficiency, but sometimes this occurs at the expense of system-wide communication and coordination. Finding solutions in the limited context of one ministry may unwittingly lead to bigger future problems for another ministry. It is

Scenario-based planning provides a common framework and language that can galvanise many agencies into thinking about the future in a systematic way.

The construction of scenarios is not an end in itself: to be useful, they must be translated into implementable strategies and plans of action.

To optimise the use of resources, the critical question is: "This is how much we have. What is the most we can get out of it?"

therefore necessary to think and work together within a common mental framework. Scenario-based planning provides this common framework and the common language that can galvanise many agencies into thinking about the future in a systematic way.

The construction of scenarios is not an end in itself: to be useful, they must be translated into implementable strategies and plans of action. It is through the process of seeking new perspectives and questioning assumptions that organisational flexibility as well as the capacity to anticipate change is built, and the ability to adapt nimbly and quickly to changing circumstances in a changing environment is developed. This is crucial for keeping Singapore competitive and cohesive into the future.

Beyond Least for Output to Most for Input: The Ministry of Finance has, over the years, increasingly devolved powers to ministries to have greater say in managing their budgets and operations. The idea of decentralisation and empowerment is based on the premise that those closest to the customer are in the best position to optimise the use of resources for serving them.

To optimise the use of resources, the critical question is: "This is how much we have. What is the most we can get out of it?" Such an optimisation approach forces priorities to be set and helps induce creativity and innovation. It is a different mind-set from the approach of: "This is what we want to do; this is how much we need."

Beyond Management to Leadership: Every organisation needs leadership, not just sound management practices and good administration. This is particularly important in the public sector where there must be an enhanced kind of leadership ability because there is no profit bottom line to warn of impending trouble, and to help communicate to workers that their livelihoods are at stake if they do not keep up with productivity improvement.

It is not easy to motivate people to deliver the best service possible when there is no competitor offering the same service and when no one else knows how much can be improved because the public does not

The public service will keep on going even with mediocre leadership, but if it aspires to be first class, it requires superior leadership.

To lead effectively, leaders need to set direction, offer guidance, and ensure that their people know the mission at hand.

The public service must go from being a mere service provider and regulator to being:

- A catalyst for change
- A standard bearer
- A pace setter that creates the path to the future, leads the way forward, and maintains a sense of urgency

know the processes and policies to be able to say how much better the service can be.

Not having a bottom line means one less instrument to encourage improvement and induce change, and also means higher demands on the quality of leadership required in the public service, as well as on the leader's ability to lead by example, communicate, and motivate.

A public service will keep on going even with mediocre leadership, but if it aspires to be first class, it requires superior leadership. To lead effectively, leaders need to set direction, offer guidance, and provide purpose by ensuring that the people know the mission at hand: what they are supposed to accomplish and why they are doing it.

Leaders must give all the support their people need to do an excellent job — this means giving them resources, tools, equipment, information, and knowledge, as well as moral support by listening, inspiring, facilitating, encouraging, and celebrating.

To develop instincts on what really matters for Singapore, enhance the quality of service and commitment to the public, and develop openness to new ideas and a future orientation in thinking, the Institute of Policy Development of the Civil Service College was specifically set up to train people for public sector leadership. The Institute focuses on the issues that will make or break Singapore: Singapore's unique situation in terms of size and location, population and demographics, multiracialism, vulnerabilities, uncertainties, and opportunities.

The public service must go from being a mere service provider and regulator to being a catalyst for change, as well as a standard bearer that is not only able to set superior standards in public service and public administration, but also match best management practices in the private sector. The public service should also be a pace setter that creates the path to the future, leads the way forward, and maintains a sense of urgency.

PS21: THE STRATEGIC IMPERATIVE

PS21 has been promoted on the basis that operations that are well executed, futures that are well anticipated, talent that is well deployed, and creativity that is well harnessed are all strategic. The theme of PS21

Four Principles for Effective Public Communication:

- **Ensure that the message can be easily understood**
- **Ensure that the message is clear**
- **Convince the public that the policy is reasoned and reasonable**
- **Start with the target audience in mind**

Each situation, each target audience, deserves careful thought. There is no substitute for empathy, and no excuse for not caring to reach out.

Communication is Intention; Implementation is Policy. What this means is that it does not matter what policy paper has been written, how well the case has been argued with the minister, or how good or clever the arguments and rationale have been. What is communicated to the audience is the intention of the policy so far as the audience is concerned. Communicate wrongly, communicate inadequately, and all the misreading and unintended distrust cannot be blamed on the audience.

Similarly, what and how the policy is implemented defines the policy. It is not what has been written in the policy paper; as far as the public is concerned, it is what they see or perceive of the implementation that defines the policy.

So there we have it: Originator, Message, Reason, and Audience. Do it right and enjoy the results. Do it wrong and be prepared for untold amounts of headache!

CHALLENGE 6

PURSUE EXCELLENCE CONSTANTLY

There is a story of a martial arts student who kneeled before the master *sensei* to receive his black belt. It was after many years of hard training.

"Before giving you the belt, you must pass one more test," the *sensei* said.

"I am ready," the student said, thinking it would be just one final lesson.

"What is the true meaning of the black belt?" the *sensei* asked.

"The end of my journey," the student said. "A good reward for all my hard work."

The *sensei* waited for more. Clearly, he was not satisfied. Finally, the *sensei* spoke. "You are not ready for the black belt. Return in one year."

A year later, the student knelt again in front of the *sensei*. "What is the true meaning of the black belt?" the *sensei* asked.

"A symbol of distinction and the highest achievement in our art," the student replied.

The *sensei* said nothing for many minutes. Clearly, he was not satisfied. Finally, he spoke. "You are still not ready for the black belt. Return in one year."

A year later, the student knelt once again in front of the *sensei*. And again the *sensei* asked: "What is the true meaning of the black belt?"

"The black belt represents the beginning — the start of a never-ending journey of discipline, hard work, and the pursuit of an ever higher standard," the student said.

"Yes. You are now ready to receive the black belt and begin your work."

As we can see, the black belt is not the highest point. The black belt is what allows us to go on to the next point.

What is your black belt? The O-levels? Or was that only to move you to the A-levels? Or is your black belt the ITE certificate? Or the polytechnic diploma? The university degree? Or the first job? Or your present job? Or is your present job only the start of working towards your future job?

What is your organisation's black belt? Is it the ISO 9000 certificate? Or the People Developer Standard? The Balanced Scorecard? The Learning Organisation? Six Sigma? The School Excellence Award? The Singapore Quality Class? The Singapore Quality Award?

You may say, "This is terrible. It never ends. We have to think and try and do and think and try and do, and it goes on and on..."

My answer: "This is why we need to believe in what we do. We need to believe it is worth doing.

We need to believe we are doing something useful. We need to find the work interesting and challenging. We need to have fun along the way.

We need to be unhappy with ourselves if we have not done our best. We need to be learning new things.

We need to find we are getting better day by day.

Otherwise life will be a big burden and work will be deadly."

I have used a lot of words. All I mean is, "Believe in yourself. Be the best you can be. Do the best you can."

Excellence is a never-ending journey. Supervisors must help make it interesting and worthwhile. But it is our attitude that will make the journey either fun or boring.

CHAPTER 6

In many organisations that believe in having a set of values to guide behaviour, managers have to deal differently with staff who exhibit differing combinations of performance and commitment to the values of the organisation.

Chapter 6

CULTURE AND VALUES

In many organisations that believe in having a set of values to guide behaviour, the question is often posed in the training of their managers as to what they would do with staff who exhibit differing combinations of performance and commitment to the values of the organisation.

Where performance and commitment to values are high, the reaction is obvious: Reward the staff and do all you can to retain them. The reaction is just as obvious for staff who are unsatisfactory in performance and do not subscribe to the values: Warn them and if they do not respond, remove them.

However, what about staff who do not offer satisfactory performance but subscribe to the values? You could retrain them to fill the gaps in their competence, or redeploy them to a position that better fits their capability, but if this does not work, you have to help the staff go somewhere else where they may better realise their potential.

The most difficult choice is where the staff offers superior performance but clearly does not subscribe to the values of the organisation; he is in his own world but does a wonderful job for the company. Oftentimes, managers will react to the situation by warning the staff and giving them every chance to behave better. This, however, only treats the symptom, so after some time, managers often find that the staff has to be "restrained" or "isolated" so that his bad behaviour does not contaminate the rest of the organisation. However, in many cases, managers find that if the staff refuses to conform to the values espoused by the organisation, the staff has to be removed and replaced. This conclusion is often reached reluctantly, because there is always the sense of unnecessary loss to have to let a high performer go.

Values are the attributes that are the fundamental factors essential for the long-term success of the company.

Values serve as the compass for the organisation.

This is a situation where the principle of meritocracy poses a real challenge: Is meritocracy about performance, or behaviour, or both? Also, which is more important?

The four combinations of performance versus values are summarised in the diagram below:

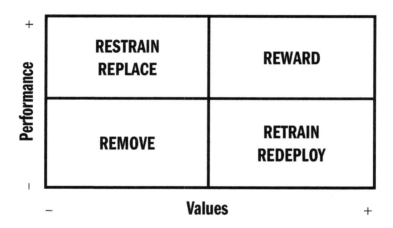

The Trade-off between Performance and Values

The interesting question is: Why is it the best choice to remove a high performing staff if their commitment to values is not commensurate with their performance? Why do values have to win?

The answer lies in understanding that values are the attributes that are the fundamental factors essential for the long-term success of the company.

In other words, values serve as the compass for the organisation as it traverses new ground for which maps have not been drawn. Values are the essential expression of the nature of the evolving organisation: they are both aspirational and essential. Hence, an organisation that declares integrity to be its value cannot compromise on any act of dishonesty or

Values are what define the character of the organisation; culture describes its current personality.

The gap between the culture and the values of an organisation represents the amount of work that has to be done to get the organisation onto its winning path.

Values do not just define organisations; they define the direction of:

- Individuals
- Families
- Companies
- Societies
- Nations

corruption, even though it may forgive oversight and poor judgment; similarly, organisations that claim service in its list of values must make no compromise on efforts to delight their customers.

Hence, while a high performer need not be removed or replaced immediately, he cannot be expected to bring the company into a successful future, as the compass by which he is operating is different from the compass that guides the organisation.

HOW "CULTURE" DIFFERS FROM "VALUES"

"Culture" is how things are today in the company. An astute observer can assess the prevailing culture by observing the behaviour of the members of the organisation: their language, their interaction, the way they treat each other and their customers, how they are appraised and rewarded, and so on. To change the culture of an organisation is to change the behaviour of everyone; this can never be achieved overnight, and in many instances, the staff who refuse to change will simply have to be removed.

"Values" are the attributes the organisation believes it should imbibe to make its future and assure its continued success. The gap between the culture and the values of an organisation represents the amount of work that has to be done to get the organisation onto its winning path; that is, if the values have been correctly identified to be what is essential for winning!

Values that are a listing of desirable traits either define the life of the organisation as it makes its way into the future or undermine integrity in the organisation because the staff are aware that the values are not taken seriously. In short, values are what define the character of the organisation, while culture describes its current personality.

But values do not just define organisations — they define the direction of individuals, families, companies, societies, and nations. The culture of societies and nations is defined by the values, behaviours, and practices expressed in the arenas of the arts and entertainment, business and economics, religion, media, education, family, and government. For example, Singapore has developed a set of five National Values:

The laws of a country should reflect the values of society that have been deemed essential for the long-term stability, prosperity, and success of the nation.

Moral education is extremely important and it starts first from the home.

"So long as you have firm convictions of what is right, what is wrong, what is good, what is bad, they will see you through."

Dr Goh Keng Swee

- Nation before community and society above self
- Family as the basic unit of society
- Community support and respect for the individual
- Consensus, not conflict
- Racial and religious harmony

The laws of a country should reflect the values of society that have been deemed essential for the long-term stability, prosperity, and success of the nation. Hence, moral education is extremely important and it starts first from the home, where the child learns through observation and discipline in his family, and then the school, which reinforces and/or refines what he has learned from his observations in his formative years.

Dr Goh Keng Swee, when he was First Deputy Prime Minister and Minister of Education, made some highly notable observations on moral education in an interview published in *The Straits Times* over three days from 28 to 30 December 1982. I quote several excerpts from the interview to underscore the importance of moral education:

- "The purpose of the moral education programme is to ensure that succeeding generations of Singaporeans will continue to know right from wrong."

- "The faithful are fortunate ... they are not only more likely to refrain from doing what they believe to be wrong, but also to have an advantage over others. Their faith helps them cope with stress and crisis, and to bring up their children properly. The agnostics, those with no religion, but who do not necessarily disbelieve in God, are not without character or resilience, provided they have strong moral principles."

- "So long as you have firm convictions of what is right, what is wrong, what is good, what is bad, they will see you through. When you examine the great religions, the basic values are very much the same. If you believe in God and you believe in your religion, good luck to you. You are very fortunate. I will never try to talk a Christian or a Hindu or a Muslim out of his religious belief. I think it would be absolutely wrong. You've got something when you have religious faith. A precious asset, isn't it?"

"As you go through life, you are bound to meet disappointments, family crises, and work stress. My observation is that those who have deep religious convictions or deep moral principles cope better than those who don't."

Dr Goh Keng Swee

- "Some people say that government is concerned only with secular matters — the economy, the banking system or whatever, employment; matters spiritual belong to the church and the bishops, and that is all right if you are a believer. I think a believing Christian is a very lucky man. He has achieved peace of mind because he believes in God and the Scriptures. I have noticed that Christians, generally speaking, conduct their lives in a very orderly way. They don't go for excitement and distractions, they don't waste money, and they raise their children very strictly according to moral principles. Their children will become moral persons, and a person with moral principles is more likely to do well than a person without such principles. So those in Singapore who have true religious faith, whether it be Christianity, or Hinduism, or Islam, or Buddhism have a decided advantage over those who don't. But having said that, there are some agnostics who develop their own moral principles. The Prime Minister (referring to then Prime Minister, Mr Lee Kuan Yew), for instance, is agnostic. But he was taught right and wrong by his grandmother. And he's a man of very strict moral principles. For that matter, so are other members of the old guard (referring to the first generation political leaders of Singapore)."

- "As you go through life, you are bound to meet disappointments, family crises, and work stress. My observation is that those who have deep religious convictions or deep moral principles cope better than those who don't. And an interesting point about this is the rise of the charismatic Christian movement. Many young business executives find it difficult to cope with the stress of competition and work. Many of them have been enlisted by the charismatic Christians, and I assume they find some benefit. But I can't say more than that."

- "There are enduring values of great civilisations and great religions, which individuals and societies can ignore and discard at their own peril. This I have learnt through years and years of experience. I can put it this way — the effect on individuals. I have noticed people

"It is moral and ethical values that determine the strength of society."

Dr Goh Keng Swee

Dr Goh Keng Swee's point in emphasising moral education was that "without morality and a sense of public duty that does not put self always first, Singapore could decline," and that it was particularly important to prevent the dilution of values from generation to generation.

who have succeeded and become rich. And those who have moral values, whether religious or non-religious, have conducted their lives in a satisfactory way. That is to say, they raised and brought up their children properly, they are not obsessed with acquiring money for the sake of acquiring money, although the rich of course do accumulate wealth. That's their main purpose. Nevertheless, they see the social obligations and try to carry them out. On the other hand, there are those who do not appear to have moral values. I find that they tend to neglect their children, and then the children sometimes end up in an awful mess."

Dr Goh's point in emphasising moral education was that "without morality and a sense of public duty that does not put self always first, Singapore could decline." He said that it was particularly important to prevent the dilution of values from generation to generation, because "we're exposed to these Western ideas, both good and bad — and usually the bad ideas are more appealing than the good ones."

Dr Goh's interview was part of the public communication process in a decision to make Religious Knowledge a compulsory subject for all upper secondary school students from 1984. They could choose any one of six religious knowledge subjects to study: Bible Knowledge, Buddhist Studies, Confucian Ethics, Hindu Studies, Islamic Religious Knowledge, or Sikh Studies.

Dr Goh believed that studying religion for its ethics was the way to produce morally upright citizens. When he introduced the idea to the public in January 1982, he shared that when he was in charge of the army, he noticed that one common occurrence in battalion camps was that if you left your wallet or watch unattended for more than ten seconds, it disappeared. "So," he continued, "one day I told the Prime Minister that the schools are turning out a nation of thieves and that something must be done about this in our education system."

Summing up his views on religious education, Dr Goh said, "The aims of this exercise are modest. We don't believe we're going to make all Singaporeans upright. Every society has its black sheep. But at least when they've gone through a course on religious knowledge, most of them will leave school believing it's wrong to lie, cheat, and steal. Many now do not."

"The teaching of religious knowledge and moral education in our schools will not solve all our problems. But if well taught it could provide an anchor in the midst of the cross currents of change which are going on around us."

Dr Tay Eng Soon

The then Minister of State for Education, Dr Tay Eng Soon, said in a speech in February 1982: "The societies and civilisations from which we have descended have all been shaped and moulded by great religions and ethical teachings. Hinduism for example has permeated through Indian culture and thought for several thousand years. The Chinese civilisation has been profoundly influenced by Confucian ethics. These civilisations have undergone great upheavals, wars, and change. It would be true to say that it was their moral and religious beliefs that have provided the continuity and given their people the strength to survive these changes.

"We would be foolish not to learn from what the great religions and ethical disciplines can teach us, especially in our present scientific and materialistic age. We can readily observe what is happening to those societies that have abandoned or lost the time-tested moral and religious beliefs of their forebears. They have become amoral; they are permissive and self-indulgent, they are also turning to all kinds of fads and cults. And the thoughtful members of their societies are worried about these trends.

"We do not want this to happen to us. The teaching of religious knowledge and ethics can certainly reinforce the moral values of our children and provide them with a moral compass for life even though we know there are many other factors such as the home, the example of elders and so on, which greatly influence the moral character of children. The teaching of religious knowledge and moral education in our schools will not solve all our problems. But if well taught it could provide an anchor in the midst of the cross currents of change which are going on around us."

The policy of compulsory religious education in upper secondary school, however, did not last. Dr Goh Keng Swee's successor as Education Minister, Dr Tony Tan, reversed it after six years. He explained to Parliament in a Ministerial Statement in October 1989 that "there is today a heightened consciousness of religious differences and a new fervour in the propagation of religious beliefs. This trend is worldwide and it embraces all faiths.

"It can be seen in the growth of Islamic fundamentalism, enhanced Christian evangelisation, and resurgence of activity and interest among

While Religious Knowledge as a compulsory subject in secondary school has ceased for more than two decades, Dr Goh's point that moral and ethical values determine the strength of society remains relevant even though trying to teach moral education without religion is, of course, very difficult.

traditional religions such as Buddhism. If carried to extremes, this trend towards greater fervour in the propagation of religious beliefs can disrupt our traditional religious harmony and religious tolerance, which are prerequisites for life in Singapore.

"It is not possible for Government to ignore this new development. We must take cognisance of it and we must implement measures to ensure that it does not upset the present climate of religious tolerance in Singapore. I think we have to face this fact squarely. But to avoid any suspicion of partiality in formulating and implementing the measures, it is essential for Government to be seen to be scrupulously neutral and even-handed in the handling of religious matters in Singapore.

"Now, to avoid any misunderstanding, I want to clarify what is meant by the phrase 'to be neutral and even-handed in the handling of religious matters.' What the phrase means simply is that Government cannot and should not be perceived to lean towards or to favour any particular religion. The phrase does not mean that Government is against religion."

Dr Tan concluded, "If we accept the principle that the proper province for the teaching of religious beliefs is not in the schools but in the home, then it must follow that Religious Knowledge should not be made a compulsory subject to be taught within curriculum time in schools. In place of the Religious Knowledge programmes, the Ministry of Education extended the Civics/Moral Education Programme, already being taught in the lower secondary school levels, to Secondary Three and Four, also incorporating aspects of nation building, an awareness of the national shared values, and an appreciation of the beliefs and practices of the various religions and races in Singapore."

While Religious Knowledge as a compulsory subject in secondary school has ceased for more than two decades, Dr Goh's point that moral and ethical values determine the strength of society remains relevant even though trying to teach moral education without religion is, of course, very difficult.

Imagine a teacher teaching his students to be kind, caring, under-standing, honest, and sincere, and the next thing that happens is that the students see him shouting at an old lady.

Teaching moral education within the context of religion would allow the teacher to say, "This is the ideal, and this is what is right and what

If we become a society where what is legal is right and what is illegal is wrong, then we would have reduced morality to the law, and thereby the whole moral fibre of society would be damaged.

is wrong. I don't care what religion you believe in but this is what your religion teaches about behaviour in society and the way to treat other people. Sometimes even I fail, but we all must keep trying to do what is right and stop doing what is wrong." However, by teaching moral education without religion, the need for personal example by the teacher is very great, and his teaching fails when the students do not see the teaching to be true for his life. The point simply is that, values, morals, and ethics are basically "caught" from family and school rather than "taught" in formal lessons and tests.

If we become a society where what is legal is right and what is illegal is wrong, then we would have reduced morality to the law, and thereby the whole moral fibre of society would be damaged. The law should be the expression of what the conscience of society and the intuition of the individual indicate to be right and good, and should set the boundary beyond which the individual will be trespassing onto the rights of others or posing a danger to them. However, when a society becomes one where the law defines what is right and what is good, the law must become tighter and tighter to tell the individual in greater and greater detail what he must do and what he must not do. The government will then become more and more autocratic, and behave more and more like a god. Accordingly, society will then weaken, as the conscience that resides in each one of us becomes silenced. Where the conscience in the individual is strong and/or where people have the fear of God — which very often is a fear of divine retribution and of what may happen to them in this life or after they die — people will behave responsibly even when there is no one to catch them and punish them. This is where religion plays a role to provide a sense of concern and responsibility for their fellowmen.

Think, for example, of the Golden Rule that Christianity teaches: "Do unto others what you would have them do to you." The same rule can be found in various ancient cultures and religions. For example, Confucius taught: "Do not impose on others what you do not desire others to impose upon you"; the Hindu sacred literature Mahabharata states: "Let no man do to another that which would be repugnant to himself"; and the Buddhist sacred literature Udanavarga says: "Hurt not others in ways you yourself would find hurtful."

Confucius said of government: "If the people are governed by laws

"If the people are governed by laws and punishment is used to maintain order, they will try to avoid the punishment but have no sense of shame. If they are governed by virtue and rules of propriety are used to maintain order, they will have a sense of shame and will become good as well."

Confucius

Government cannot motivate people from within as to what is right and good.

Only religion or high moral values in the heart can move people to act beyond self-interest and move society to a higher level of care and concern, as well as a deeper sense of community and social responsibility.

and punishment is used to maintain order, they will try to avoid the punishment but have no sense of shame. If they are governed by virtue and rules of propriety are used to maintain order, they will have a sense of shame and will become good as well."[3]

Government cannot keep alive the conscience in each one of us and motivate people from within as to what is right and good. The law and the policeman are there to prevent people from doing what is irresponsible towards others. Only religion or high moral values in the heart can move people to act beyond self-interest and move society to a higher level of care and concern, as well as a deeper sense of community and social responsibility.

As mentioned in a previous chapter, my personal view is that the next phase of development of the Singapore education system should be what I might call "values-driven."

By values, I mean something much wider than personal and social values, and even wider than the National Values that had been approved by Parliament in 1991 — values that were developed to meet the three objectives of finding common values that all can share, preserving the heritage of the different communities, and ensuring that each community also appreciates and is sensitive to the traditions of others. Neither do I mean values about national independence and sovereignty borne in the five aspects of Total Defence — Military Defence, Civil Defence, Economic Defence, Social Defence, and Psychological Defence — and expressed in the six National Education Messages.

While all these thoughts, messages, and beliefs are essential and critical, I believe we now have to build on them and go beyond them for the sake of our children. The next phase in the development of the Singapore education system should build upon everything that is good and beneficial in the previous three phases. This "values-driven" phase would take us the next step in the drive to encourage each child to be the best he or she can be.

When I speak of "values-driven education" for our children in school, I am thinking of what it is in their beliefs, perspectives, attitudes, and

---

[3] The Analects 2.3.

Values-driven education addresses the questions of:

- **Identity: "Who am I?"**
- **Community: "What can I do?"**
- **Discovery: "What can I be?"**

"Nations have no permanent friends or allies; they only have permanent interests."

Lord Palmerston

There is a need to continually think and debate how Singapore is to continually succeed.

fundamental motivations that would empower them best for their lives in future. I would list these as:

- **Values of Identity**
- **Values of Community**
- **Values of Discovery**

First, our young need a strong sense of identity. They need to feel comfortable with themselves and have a sense of belonging to their family, to their community, and to their country. "Values of Identity" basically answer the question, "Who am I?" This is grounded in one's character, personality, morals, and ethics, and is also derived from family, religion, language, culture, and country.

If "Values of Identity" address the question, "Who am I?" "Values of Community" address the question, "What can I do?" Our children need to have "Values of Community" so that they can get on with others and have a strong sense of social and moral responsibility. It is important to develop the emotional quotient (EQ) of our children to enable them to work with and through others, and imbibe in them the values of integrity, other-centredness, harmony, and trustworthiness. It is about understanding what is good for the public at large, and holding the government accountable to ensure that it fulfils its role of assuring justice, security, stability, and the rule of law, as well as establishing and maintaining the supporting social and legal institutions to assure the public good. Above all, it is about the individual doing his or her part for others and for his or her country, if not driven by "love," then at least by what Dr Goh Keng Swee often referred to as "enlightened self-interest."

In a way, the concept of "Values of Identity" and "Values of Community" are nothing new; schools have been working on them since Singapore's independence. But I believe they have to be given a new impetus because a generation of children and their teachers have grown up without living through the struggle, drama, doubts, and fears of the early years. There is a need to continually think and debate how Singapore is to continually succeed in the real world. As succinctly described by Lord Henry Palmerston, the English statesman of the 19th century (1784–1865): "Nations have no permanent friends or allies; they only have permanent interests."

The greatest threat to the continuing success and national well-being of Singapore is the lack of entrepreneurs, innovators, researchers, and leaders.

Beyond these first and second sets of values should be a third set of values that I think are underdeveloped in Singapore. Our children need to have "Values of Discovery" so that instead of being told facts and conclusions, they find things out and think things through for themselves.

"Values of Discovery" would lead one to maintain a sense of constant curiosity, take the initiative to learn by doing, have the courage to be different, be willing to try and to learn from mistakes, and have a sense of adventure, dedication, persistence, and determination, as well as a relentless drive for excellence.

We often lament a lack of innovative spirit among Singaporeans, and accept too easily the analysis of outside commentators who say that this situation has arisen because Singaporean children are brought up to conform and are too scared to question. I think the reason Singaporean kids simply go along is because they have been taught to be smart and efficient, and they think the smart and efficient thing to do is to go with the herd, and keep to the tried and tested path. We have to change this.

We often talk of Singaporeans lacking creativity, as though this is something we can deliver through rules and methods. I do not think it is a matter of methods — if it were just a matter of methods, we would certainly have little difficulty achieving creativity in our schools with all our capability in curriculum development, peer sharing, and so on. I think this is fundamentally an issue of building up courage, confidence, energy, and imagination in every child. To achieve this, it has to be the passionate desire of teachers to have all their students be the best they can be in all areas of their lives, and help them discover themselves not just in their capacity to acquire and apply knowledge and skills, but also in the desire to pursue, to explore, to invent, to uncover, to be all that they were made to be.

As I contemplate the future for Singapore, I think our greatest threat to continuing success and national well-being is the lack of entrepreneurs, innovators, researchers, and leaders. Entrepreneurs build businesses that would never exist without them; innovators do things differently from how they have always been done; researchers discover things never known before; and leaders make things happen that would otherwise not happen on their own.

In every instance, the driving force of energy and imagination is to

It is the courage and confidence to be different that brings success.

If we are to foster a spirit of inquiry and enterprise in our students, teachers must be the prime source of encouragement for students to build their courage and confidence to try, to learn, to create, to destroy, to pursue, and to fail.

Teachers have to figure out how to let their students taste success as they try and learn, for this is what builds up courage and confidence, and drives motivation, energy, and imagination.

bring about something new and something different, whether this be in the public or the private sector, and it is the confidence and courage to be different that brings success.

To be different is not the same as being contrarian: it is knowing why you believe what you are believing, and why you are doing what you are doing. Sometimes it is putting things together in a different way than how others have been doing, sometimes it is doing what others have never done before, and sometimes it is doing what others are doing but more effectively, more efficiently, and more effortlessly.

If we are to foster such a spirit of inquiry and enterprise in our students, teachers must be the prime source of encouragement for students to build their courage and confidence to try, to learn, to create, to destroy, to pursue, and to fail. This is not a matter of simply delivering lessons in life skills, but a way of thinking and living by learning and doing.

It was in the Ministry of Education that I learnt there were things that have to be "caught and not taught." This certainly is a critical area that children have to learn by "catching" from their teachers: for children to grow to be "like that," the teachers have first to be "like that" too. Teachers have to figure out how to let their students taste success as they try and learn, for this is what builds up courage and confidence, and drives motivation, energy, and imagination.

If "Values of Identity" address the question, "Who am I?" and "Values of Community" address the question, "What can I do?" then "Values of Discovery" address the question, "What can I be?"

I have a picture hanging in my office painted by my first granddaughter when she was five. It is a rather big picture of a sheep in the pasture with a fence, a blue sky with a shining sun and cotton-wool clouds. However, contrary to convention, the sheep is red with purple ears, one cloud is blue, and the other is white. The picture is alive with all kinds of colours but a few adults have a problem with the red sheep, purple ears, and blue clouds. I hang the picture in my room because it is a continuing inspiration for me and all who come to my office: Look at the colours and lift up your spirit, come alive, and do not be inhibited by what others think — this must be the way things have to be.

The role of the teacher is evolving. It is no longer good enough for a teacher to just transmit facts and information; a teacher has to teach the

While a teacher has a significant influence on the development of the child's attitude for the rest of his or her life, the starting point always has to be the child's parents and family.

As much of a child's attitude is instilled before he or she even goes to school, family involvement must be part of any values-driven education.

Singaporeans cannot afford to rest on the achievements of the past.

Singapore must build its business competitiveness on the values of integrity, quality, reliability, imagination, responsiveness, and an unending drive for excellence.

We are no longer a low cost base. The battle must be fought on a different plane.

students how to fish rather than simply provide the student with fish. A teacher has to teach social skills, demonstrate moral behaviour, build confidence, yet invoke humility. A teacher also has to teach the students how to differentiate good from bad, do what is right, and right the wrongs. In short, a teacher plays a significant role in inculcating the "Values of Identity," "Values of Community," and, most importantly, the "Values of Discovery," in every child.

However, while a teacher has a significant influence on the development of the child's attitude for the rest of his or her life, the starting point always has to be the child's parents and family. Much research has shown that if parents are involved in their child's education, the child will learn more, and while parents can delegate the role of teaching to the school, they must support what the school does, otherwise the school would be operating without legitimate authority over their children.

More fundamentally, as much of a child's attitude is instilled before he or she even goes to school, family involvement must be part of any "values-driven" education as the education of every child starts from the home.

VALUES IN BUSINESS

Finally, some thoughts on values in business.

Singapore has made the leap from Third World to First World in little more than a generation. It is a remarkable achievement by any standard. But that is the past; Singaporeans cannot afford to rest on the achievements of the past.

Cost factors, social stresses, demographic changes, the aspirations of youth, and, most of all, a whole world of people and nations wishing to improve their standards of living demand a continuous questioning of Singapore's value proposition in a world of self-interested nations.

Economic opportunity is what keeps hope flowing and energy levels high — such growth requires a thriving private sector of enterprises with a global outlook led by leaders with imagination and courage. I posit that Singapore must build its business competitiveness on the values of integrity, quality, reliability, imagination, responsiveness, and an unending drive for excellence. We are no longer a low cost base. The battle must be

Singapore has to go the way of being a five-star business. There will be technologies to be learnt and methodology to be acquired, but the fundamental driver of success has to be the right values.

fought on a different plane. The values I have listed have to be part of the psyche of workers and leaders in business, and that psyche has to be built from young, fostered by families, and reinforced in school.

IN CLOSING...

I close with a story of imagination and possibilities, a true story for which the actors cannot be named.

There was a businessman in China who became convinced after he became a Christian that the way he had been conducting his business was wrong; his conscience had come alive and he decided that he had to change course.

This businessman called his top manager and said that the company had to stop paying bribes. His manager told him that this would be a most irresponsible thing to do: his decision would jeopardise the livelihood of all his workers, as the way they had been getting their sales was through bribery. This was a most unexpected reaction, as the businessman thought it would be plain that giving bribes was wrong.

He thought over the dilemma of his people and wisdom came to him. He told his staff, "We are going to change the nature of our business. If we were running a hotel business, we can choose either to be a one-star hotel business or a five-star hotel business. If we are a one-star hotel business, we will be competing on cost by all ways and means. If we are a five-star hotel business, we will be fighting for business based on quality, reliability, and customer service." He then said, "We are going to change our business to the five-star model."

Think about Singapore. Singapore has to go the way of being a five-star business. There will be technologies to be learnt and methodology to be acquired, but the fundamental driver of success has to be the right values.

CHALLENGE 7

LEARN TO BE A PART OF AN ORCHESTRA

Imagine an orchestra. It can be a symphony orchestra, a Chinese orchestra, or any other type of orchestra.

There is a whole range of instruments. Each instrument makes its own sound. In a symphony orchestra, the strings, such as the violin, cello, and harp are the most versatile and flexible. The woodwinds, such as the flute and clarinet, add colour and melody. The brass, such as the trumpet and trombone, often provide dramatic climax. The percussion instruments, such as the drums, triangle, and xylophone, give the music a rhythmic feel.

While each instrument makes its own sound, it is silly to say one is more important than the other. The fact is that by joining the sounds together, we get wonderful music.

Take out any of the instruments, and the orchestra loses something in its music. Indeed, take out one violin, and the orchestra loses something even though there may be another 19 violins still playing.

There is also a conductor. He is the one who brings the instruments together so that every musician plays his part well — when to come in, how loud to play, how fast to play, when to stop playing, and so on. The orchestra needs him even though he does not play anything during the performance.

The musicians come together in an orchestra because they want to make marvellous music. This is not possible with each one just playing on his or her own.

Every player is an expert with regards to his instrument. But he has to pay attention to the conductor, to see and hear what other members of the orchestra are doing, and to blend his instrument into the total effort. Only total cooperation can produce wonderful results.

We should see our work in the office as though we are players in an orchestra.

Each of us must know what we are doing. We must have the skills, expertise, and knowledge, and we must be prepared to keep learning and improving our abilities.

At the same time we must know what others are doing, so that we can blend our work with theirs to produce first-class total results.

We must respect others for their abilities. If all of us were the same, we would produce poorer results than by joining together to make the most use of our different strengths.

PART II
THE LEADER

CHAPTER 7

Unless there is a codification of values and principles of successful leadership, and a regular re-expression of the values and principles in ways relevant to each generation, all organisations will suffer the consequences of atrophy and entropy.

Organisations often fall victim to one of three kinds of fatal failure:

- A failure to learn from the past
- A failure to adapt to the present
- A failure to anticipate the future

Chapter 7

LEADERSHIP

The Chinese have a saying "富不过三代" or "Wealth does not last beyond three generations." The first generation builds the wealth, the second generation maintains the wealth, while the third generation squanders away the wealth.

The same happens in the leadership of organisations: The first generation defines successful leadership by their values and actions, the second generation learns leadership by imbibing relevant lessons and keeping relevant practices, and the third generation fails in the leadership of the organisation because the second generation has transmitted only a truncated part of the values and lessons of successful leadership from the first generation.

My point is a simple one: Unless there is a codification of values and principles of successful leadership, and a regular re-expression of the values and principles in ways relevant to each generation, all organisations will suffer the consequences of atrophy and entropy.

Organisations often fall victim to one of three kinds of fatal failure:

- A failure to learn from the past
- A failure to adapt to the present
- A failure to anticipate the future

The challenge is to have leadership that is both confident as well as humble, a leadership knowledgeable of the past yet questioning about the future, and a leadership never satisfied with today's achievements because complacency is fatal for tomorrow's success.

I have had a very good run of opportunities to make a difference

Three Leadership Imperatives:

- Be the Best You Can Be
- Harness the Creativity of Your People
- Be in Time for the Future

Leadership is making things happen that on their own would not happen.

Every leader has to master:

- Position Leadership
- Personal Leadership

in every place I have been due to what I believe is divine providence. Everything I have sought to do in all these places can be summarised in three imperatives:

- **Be the Best You Can Be**
- **Harness the Creativity of Your People**
- **Be in Time for the Future**

The first two pertain to the stewardship of talents and abilities that every individual has.

- **"Be the Best You Can Be"** is a call to the individual to do one's best and to be all he or she can be. It is a matter of motivation, attitude, and humility to learn and to serve.

- **"Harness the Creativity of Your People"** is a call to supervisors to allow their people to exercise their talents and abilities the best way possible, to discover themselves, to build up their self-confidence, and to enhance their ability to contribute.

- **"Be in Time for the Future"** is a rallying call to be alert, never to be complacent, and to always be actively preparing for an uncertain future.

WHAT IS LEADERSHIP

Leadership is making things happen that on their own would not happen. It is fundamentally a matter of bringing about change that is useful for the present and essential for the future. It is about being clear of the change we want and/or need to bring about, and being smart about the way we bring about change that is beneficial, effective, and enduring.

There are two aspects of leadership we have to master to be an outstanding leader:

- **Position Leadership** is the leadership that is expected of someone in the appointment that one holds.
- **Personal Leadership** is the kind of leadership that causes people to respect and want to follow a leader, not because they have to,

Position Leadership is above all about preparing and shaping the company for the future.

The full depth of one's leadership is what continues in the organisation when one is no longer around.

but but because they want to. It can be exercised by anyone at any level in an organisation.

POSITION LEADERSHIP

Position Leadership requires us to be clear about the purpose and direction for our organisation or company. It requires the leader to:

- Express the mission of the organisation
- Establish the vision of what it should become
- Define the strategy for the organisation
- Identify the needs for the effective execution of one's plans
- Define the culture and the values that are essential for sustained success of the company

Above all, Position Leadership is about preparing and shaping the company for the future because, when all is said and done, the ultimate evidence of failed leadership is the failure of an organisation to meet the challenges of the ever-changing future and to sustain its success.

In a strange kind of way, the full depth of our leadership does not lie in the day-to-day decisions we make to keep the organisation going, but what continues in the organisation when we are no longer around.

It is absolutely essential for organisations to change in good time and in good times. In a highly globalised world, the winners are those who are alert, agile, innovative, responsive, and enterprising; these winners are constantly on the lookout for dangers and opportunities.

Leaders must seek all the time to make sure that their organisations are "in time for the future" by ensuring that the company has the strategic perspective, market awareness, equipment, technology, ambition, imagination, as well as the human capital to be sustainably successful moving into the future.

There is an old African saying that goes: "Every day the gazelle wakes up knowing that if it can't outrun the fastest lion, it's going to be somebody's breakfast. Every day the lion wakes up knowing that if it can't outrun the slowest gazelle it will go hungry."

Often when I quote this proverb to urge people to make sure their

Resistance to change is normal. In fact, we should worry if we do not get resistance, because it either means that people are not taking the change seriously, or they think we will give up easily and so there is no need for them to apply themselves.

Personal Leadership is what makes Position Leadership succeed.

Personal Leadership is above all a matter of the heart.

companies are always fit to run, they enter into an argument as to whether their company is the lion or the gazelle. It actually does not matter whether your organisation is the lion or the gazelle; when morning comes, you had better be running.

That said, it matters a lot whether you are running as Number Two, following the leader's every move, or as Number One with no leader to follow and having to create your own way.

Anyone who has tried to drive change in organisations knows that it is not straightforward. Resistance to change is normal. In fact, we should worry if we do not get resistance, because it either means that people are not taking the change seriously, or they think we will give up easily and so there is no need for them to apply themselves. In other words, they believe they can outlast our ideas or outlast us!

Nevertheless, I believe that if we are determined and smart in our approach, we will be able to succeed in lowering the resistance or finding ways around the resistance. However, the hard truth is that there will be times when we may have to remove a few people who simply keep resisting and instigating other people not to support the change.

PERSONAL LEADERSHIP

Personal Leadership is what makes Position Leadership succeed. It is a matter of the heart and the mind, and makes people want to follow you because there is something worthy about your abilities, about your consideration for your staff's well-being, and about your example, which moves them to be the best they can be.

If we do not have followers, we are not a leader. We may be called Chairman or CEO or Director or Commander, but we are not a leader unless we have willing followers. People very often ask: "What do I need to do to be a good leader?" The answer is simple. One just needs to answer the question: "What would make me personally want to follow someone?"

Personal leadership is above all a matter of the heart: skills can be taught and learnt, but helping others be the best they can be is a matter

The most important question for great leadership: "How can I help you do your job better?"

of the heart. Everything revolves around what I consider to be the most important question for great leadership: "How can I help you do your job better?" If you do not remember anything else about being a leader, just remember this.

CHALLENGE 8

CONSTANTLY PREPARE FOR THE FUTURE

How to Boil a Frog

To boil a frog, do not put it in boiling water. It will jump out immediately.

Put the live frog in cold water in a pan. Put the pan over a low fire. Let the water heat up slowly. As it gets to boiling point, you will notice the frog is no longer moving. It is dead. You have successfully cooked the frog by boiling.

Explanation

I am told the above instructions work because frogs are cold-blooded — this means their body temperature is the same as the surroundings, unlike us human beings. We are warm-blooded, meaning our body temperature remains more or less constant, and does not follow that of our surroundings. We shiver in cold weather to keep our body temperature up. We sweat in warm weather to cool ourselves down.

The frog's body temperature follows its surroundings. If you put the frog directly in boiling water, it will sense the heat immediately and jump out. But when you heat the water slowly, the frog keeps adjusting to the rising temperature. When the heat is too much for the frog to take, it is too late. The frog collapses and dies.

Fatal Failures

All fatal failures in organisations are the result of failure to learn from the past, failure to adapt to the present or failure to anticipate the future.

Look at the history of nations and companies. Study wars and battles, crises and bankruptcies. Isn't it so?

Failure to learn from the past is failure to learn from mistakes — your own mistakes as well as the mistakes of others. It is best to learn from others' mistakes, but often people are not satisfied until they make the same mistakes themselves.

Failure to adapt to the present is failure to see that the practices of the past are no longer the best. The rules and practices must be brought up to date. When conditions change, organisations must change also.

Failure to anticipate the future is the most frequent cause of failure. The more successful an organisation, the greater the chances its people will be so proud and comfortable they are surprised by events they have not prepared for. Success today does not guarantee success tomorrow.

The Lesson of the Frog

Think again about the frog. Its body temperature keeps adapting to the surrounding slow change in temperature. The frog does not realise that the temperature can rise so high that it will collapse under the heat. It feels nice and comfortable at this point on the road to death.

The lesson of the frog for us is this: Look around. Be alert. Imagine the future. Don't be complacent. Take precautions. Prepare for danger. Make use of the opportunities. The future will surprise you only if you don't bother to think about it. Do not allow the comforts of today to lull you into thinking tomorrow will always be the same. Change in good time. Change in good times.

CHAPTER 8

Every organisation must have a clear sense of its mission and every management team must have a clear idea of its vision.

"Excellence" has to be understood in terms of performance relative to potential, rather than simply performance relative to the past or to peers.

Chapter 8

THE PURSUIT OF EXCELLENCE

E very organisation must have a clear sense of its mission and every management team must have a clear idea of its vision.

In all my appointments, I have led my teams and encouraged my staff to always reach out for excellence. By "excellence," I mean achieving the best performance for and by the individual, and also for and by the organisation. It is my view that "excellence" has to be understood in terms of performance relative to potential, rather than simply performance relative to the past or to peers.

Many organisations seek to improve themselves by driving for efficiency or the highest possible ratio of desired outputs to committed inputs. Others go a step further, and seek to improve themselves by driving for effectiveness or the highest possible ratio of good outcomes to committed effort. But the best organisations will seek to improve themselves by driving for the best possible performance compared to the potential of the organisation.

You will notice that the measures of efficiency, effectiveness, and excellence are different. More than that, they require fundamentally different mind-sets to achieve.

Those who are parents will know that from time to time you get upset with your children for not trying or doing their best in any assignment or examination. Many parents can accept that their children may not be the most brilliant in school or the most talented in music, but what they cannot accept is misuse, disuse, or underuse of the talent the children have, whether it be due to lack of discipline in their children or an unwillingness to apply themselves.

It is strange that people often do not measure themselves against the

It is strange that people often do not measure themselves against the same high standards of performance versus potential as they measure their children!

The need for Transcendence — that is, helping others reach their personal growth and self-fulfilment — has been ranked as the highest of all needs in the human psyche.

same high standards of performance versus potential as they measure their children. And it is just as strange or regretful that organisations often do not measure themselves or their people in terms of performance versus potential, but simply in terms of performance against targets or the previous year's results.

MASLOW'S HIERARCHY OF NEEDS

Many would have heard of Maslow's Hierarchy of Needs, where he hypothesized that the needs of human beings lie in a hierarchy where once one level of needs is met, the next higher level of needs gains prominence. Maslow identified five levels of needs:

- Biological and Physiological Needs (e.g. food, air, water, shelter)
- Safety Needs (e.g. security, stability, law)
- Love Needs (e.g. family, friends, a sense of belonging)
- Esteem Needs (e.g. status, reputation, achievement)
- Self-Actualisation Needs (e.g. the realisation of one's potential)

Not everyone agrees with Maslow's thesis, though most of the argument has been about whether the various needs actually fall in a hierarchy, or is in fact present all the time though in varying degrees for people in different circumstances or situations. However, it is interesting to note that further research in this field concludes that human beings also have:

- Cognitive Needs (e.g. understanding)
- Aesthetic Needs (e.g. beauty, balance)
- Transcendence Needs (i.e. helping others realise their potential)

Placed in order, the eight needs then stack up as:

- Biological and Physiological Needs
- Safety Needs
- Love Needs
- Esteem Needs

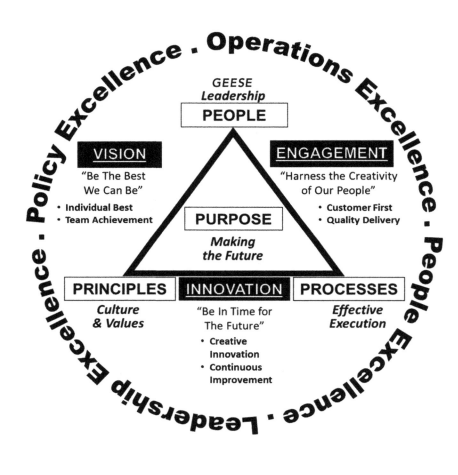

THE CIRCLE OF EXCELLENCE

- Cognitive Needs
- Aesthetic Needs
- Self-Actualisation Needs
- Transcendance Needs

The first four needs are often referred to as "gap needs." This means that people feel deficient and incapable if they lack them. The last four needs may be referred to as "growth needs," where people sense the imperative to reach beyond their current selves towards their potential.

It is very interesting that the need for Transcendence — that is, helping others reach their personal growth and self-fulfilment — has been ranked as the highest of all needs in the human psyche.

The Circle of Excellence presented in the next section is a framework to guide individuals and organisations achieve high performance today and constantly pursue their maximum potential.

THE CIRCLE OF EXCELLENCE

As seen in the diagram on the left, the centre of the Circle of Excellence comprises Four P's:

- **Purpose**
- **People**
- **Principles**
- **Processes**

Purpose: At the core of the Circle of Excellence is Purpose or Mission. What does the organisation exist for? What is the reason for its being? Some people speak of Mission following Vision, while others speak of Vision following Mission. I believe firmly that Vision must follow Mission, as Mission is something that remains in place year after year, even decade after decade. If ever the Purpose or Mission changes, it means the reason for the existence of the organisation has changed.

Once we are clear about the Mission that defines the reason for the organisation's existence over an extended period of time, it also means that the Purpose must be intuitively enduring in one or more aspects.

People conceive the future and determine what is possible; they make things happen, or not happen!

The key to bringing out the best in People lies in leadership that inspires them to be the best that they can be.

Everyone in an organisation has talent, though the nature and extent of the talent would vary from person to person.

The expression "Making the Future" illustrates that clarity of purpose is a necessary starting point to bring everyone in the organisation together and motivate them to continuously create a future for everyone. In light of this, the Purpose has to be motivating, challenging, aspirational, noble, and future-oriented.

People: People conceive the future and determine what is possible; they make things happen, or *not* happen! Motivated people will give their best, while unmotivated people will sap the energy of the organisation.

The key to bringing out the best in People lies in leadership — leadership that inspires people to push themselves to be the best that they can be. Leadership is such a critical factor that I am devoting the two subsequent chapters to discuss its two aspects of Position Leadership and Personal Leadership.

A word about talent is important at this point. Talent, to me, is the capacity each person has to realise his full potential: it is what determines how much knowledge a person may imbibe, what skills he may master, what understanding he may develop, and what experience he may build up. But all these would come to nought if he does not have the motivation to develop his potential, contribute his best, and to do it with the integrity that engenders trust and builds credibility.

Everyone in an organisation has talent, though the nature and extent of the talent would vary from person to person. Organisations need to be focussed on how to draw out the most from the talent they have, and to apply the talent in a way that best meets the organisation's purpose and best develops the individual.

A critical point about talent is whether the organisation sees it in terms of a flow of talent through the organisation, or a stock of talent in the organisation.

When leaders think of talent as a stock, they have to be careful not to run into organisational atrophy, which occurs when the same people staying in the same position for too long make it difficult for new ideas to come through in response to the changing environment, as well as new challenges and opportunities.

When leaders think of talent in terms of a flow, they would be continually thinking of how best to deploy the talent they have, how best

The key factors if the organisation thinks in terms of *flow* of talent are energy and imagination, while the key factors if the organisation thinks in terms of *stock* of talent are knowledge and experience.

It is often wrongly perceived that promotion is a reward for performance.

Promotion must always be an expectation of the probability of high performance at the next higher level.

The right reward for high performance is a good bonus.

to harness the most of their capabilities wherever they may be, and how to keep their people continually motivated by opportunities to learn and to contribute.

The key factors if the organisation thinks in terms of flow of talent are energy and imagination, while the key factors if the organisation thinks in terms of stock of talent are knowledge and experience. Provided the organisation positions itself to be able to continually recruit some of the best people for the job, energy will virtually always win over experience.

Organisations that are focussed on the potential of their people behave fundamentally differently from organisations that are focussed on the performance of their people. Performance today is absolutely essential — no matter how high the potential of a person may be, he must be rewarded only to the level of his performance. Anything other than reward for performance undermines the principle of merit and demotivates everyone else in the organisation by a process that is seen, quite correctly, as unjust and unfair. But if someone of high potential also puts in high performance, then not only would reward for performance today be fair, but also promotion for contribution at a higher level tomorrow would be justified.

It is often wrongly perceived that promotion is a reward for performance — promotion must always be an expectation of the probability of high performance at the next higher level. The right reward for high performance is a good bonus, not a promotion. No one should be promoted without good grounds to believe that the individual would perform well at the next higher level; to promote without the requisite potential for high performance is to do injustice to the individual as well as to the organisation.

At the same time, promotion must always first demand integrity, as expressed by Dee Hock, Founder of Visa International:

"Hire and promote first on the basis of integrity; second, motivation; third, capacity; fourth, understanding; fifth, knowledge; and last and least, experience. Without integrity, motivation is dangerous; without motivation, capacity is impotent; without capacity, understanding is limited; without understanding, knowledge is meaningless; without knowledge,

"Hire and promote first on the basis of integrity; second, motivation; third, capacity; fourth, understanding; fifth, knowledge; and last and least, experience.

Without integrity, motivation is dangerous; without motivation, capacity is impotent; without capacity, understanding is limited; without understanding, knowledge is meaningless; without knowledge, experience is blind.

Experience is easy to provide and quickly put to good use by people with all the other qualities."

Dee Hock

Moving people based on potential backed by performance is the fairest way to treat existing staff.

The only way to actually discover whether assessments of potential are correct is to put the person into the job.

experience is blind. Experience is easy to provide and quickly put to good use by people with all the other qualities."

Managers are often unwilling to appoint people to jobs based on their potential — they tend to look for someone who has had good experience for the job. This may well be appropriate, but has two dangers: one is that this very approach of "risk avoidance" may mean appointing a person who is good for the job today, but who cannot develop the job for tomorrow; second, it may well deny existing staff the opportunity to be stretched and tried in a new appointment because there could be a tendency to simply hire someone experienced from outside to "fill the gap," and in so doing, the danger of cultural misfit rises, and the opportunity to motivate and advance existing staff is missed.

Moving people based on potential backed by performance is the fairest way to treat existing staff and creates a good way for younger staff who are more capable and energised to advance, in an open and organised fashion, relative to less capable and less motivated staff who may have been in the organisation longer.

It requires organisational discipline to be focussed on talent and capacity, to continually assess and develop potential, and to do so in a way that recognises that all assessments of potential must be continually tentative.

The only way to actually discover whether the assessments are correct is to put the person into the job. No doubt, the person may fail. It is a risk, but it is a risk well worth taking, and absolutely necessary to take in a fast changing, dynamically challenging world where nimbleness, flexibility, creativity, innovativeness, and courage are keys to sustained organisational success.

Principles: Principles refer to what, why, and how an organisation thinks. It is a generic term that covers the thought process and encompasses culture, values, plans, strategies, and policies.

Processes: Processes refer to what, why, and how the organisation gets things done. It is a generic term that covers the execution process with the requisite attention to responsiveness, flexibility, appropriateness, quality, consistency, and reliability.

- **VISION links People and Principles**
- **ENGAGEMENT links People and Processes**
- **INNOVATION links Principles and Processes**

INTERCONNECTIONS BETWEEN THE 3P'S OF PEOPLE, PRINCIPLES, AND PROCESSES

Next, I would like to discuss the interconnections between the 3P's of People, Principles, and Processes, bearing in mind that everything that is thought and done must be justified by the Purpose of the organisation.

VISION: LINKS PEOPLE AND PRINCIPLES

Vision is the collection of ideas of what the organisation should seek to be like: it expresses the continued present and the desired future, and arises from People thinking through their hopes and aspirations based on the Principles.

ENGAGEMENT: LINKS PEOPLE AND PROCESSES

The challenge that all organisations face is how its People will implement the ideas properly and thoroughly through the Processes. The question here is how engaged the People will be in what they do: are their "hands and feet" doing merely what they are told to do, or do we also have their "hearts and minds" — a full emotional and mental commitment to the challenges at hand through total Engagement?

INNOVATION: THE LINK BETWEEN PRINCIPLES AND PROCESSES

How the Principles are translated into Processes in a dynamic way so the organisation does not get paralysed by the unexpected, and positions itself upfront for the opportunities that the future invariably offers with its uncertainties, depends on the innovative spirit that exists within the organisation. Innovation ensures that the organisation is not stuck in the past or even the present, but is always ready to change to take advantage of and create the future

CALL TO ACTION

These three elements — Vision (connecting People with Principles), Engagement (connecting People with Processes), and Innovation

Three Critical Calls to Action:

- **For Vision: Be the Best We Can Be**
- **For Engagement: Harness the Creativity of Our People**
- **For Innovation: Be in Time for the Future**

To "Be the Best We Can Be" entails three elements:

- **Each person in the organisation *doing* the best he or she can**
- **Each person in the organisation *being* the best he or she can be**
- **Everyone in the organisation *working* together for the best results**

(connecting Principles with Processes) — are what will set high performing organisations apart from mediocre ones.

Against each element there is a critical call to action:

For Vision: **Be the Best We Can Be**
For Engagement: **Harness the Creativity of Our People**
For Innovation: **Be in Time for the Future**

HAVE THE VISION TO BE THE BEST YOU CAN BE: The goal to "Be the Best We Can Be" is put forward as a generic theme. Organisations have to evolve their own specific vision, but anything less than striving to be the best it can be must mean an organisation is less than what it is capable of being.

The drive to be the best is an evergreen challenge that never expires. An organisation may even already be acknowledged to be the best in its class, but once it believes it already is the best, the process of atrophy will take over.

This call to action entails three elements:

- Each person in the organisation *doing* **the best he or she can**: This is an issue of morale and motivation.

- Each person in the organisation *being* **the best he or she can be**: This is an issue of capacity and capability, helping everyone in the organisation realise his potential the best way he can.

- Everyone in the organisation **working together for the best results**: This is an issue of synergy and symbiosis.

No organisation can be the best it can be if these three elements are not well honed. It is a call for individual best and team achievement, but above all, it is a critical call for leadership.

Visualise three characters: the first, an old man with his large walking stick, the second, a policeman with his heavy truncheon, and the third, a conductor of an orchestra with his little baton. The old man has lost all energy and control: people run circles around him, and he cannot

Engage your people to harness their creativity, create energy, and lift their spirits high.

When hearts and minds are fully engaged, individuals will feel good about themselves and be motivated to give their best — only then may the full capacity of the organisation be realised.

do anything about it. The policeman demands order through threats of penalty: people will get in line and not get on the wrong side of him. The conductor knows every instrument in the orchestra, extracts the best he can from each musician, and have them harmonise so that the orchestra produces great music. The conductor has the smallest stick of all, but creates the greatest effect by fully harnessing the totality of the creativity and capability of his musicians.

ENGAGE YOUR PEOPLE TO HARNESS THEIR CREATIVITY: As for the imperative to "Harness the Creativity of Our People," an organisation has to believe that its people are creative or innovative, or you can be sure they will never be!

If the leadership in an organisation does not believe in its people, it will not establish the conditions and systems for them to show what they are capable of. At the same time, if people do not believe that an organisation will appreciate or reward them for fully engaging their hearts and minds, people will not exercise initiative and the organisation will be poorer for it.

It is thus important to engage your people to create energy and lift their spirits high. When hearts and minds are fully engaged, individuals will feel good about themselves and be motivated to give their best — only then may the full capacity of the organisation be realised.

Suppose I were to ask you, "How many balls can you juggle at any one time?" For me, if I can do three, I will do very well. Perhaps you can do four or five, if you are not a professional juggler.

Now let us ask ourselves, "How many major tasks can we handle at any one time?" Three would be nice, four would be quite good, and five would be outstanding. So if all we want from our people is to undertake tasks directly and immediately related to our personal task list, the most we can hope for our department to accomplish by the end of the year is just the three, four, or five things.

But consider the case when we can engage our people and give them the leeway to exercise their initiative to improve things under their sphere: Even if our people are less capable than we are and can therefore handle just two important tasks each, and suppose there are ten persons under our charge in our department, by the end of the year, our department would have had 23 improvements, and not just three or four or five! This

Innovate to be in time for the future.

In order to be in time for the future, an organisation needs to be always questioning, open to new ideas, and willing to learn from anywhere.

This requires a confident, courageous, and humble leadership that is able to engage in a debate over ideas without sinking into a battle of personalities.

is the multiplier principle we should seek in the Engagement paradigm.

It has been said that the Japanese discover more comets each year than any other nation. As explained by a Japanese professor this is because the Japanese are equipped with good instruments, but more importantly, because many of its people are looking out for comets!

Clearly, having many people passionately pursuing a common end, empowering them to exercise initiative and to experiment, and giving them time and resources to venture, is a powerful combination that will result in productivity, creativity, and innovation.

INNOVATE TO BE IN TIME FOR THE FUTURE: Finally, the call to "Be in Time for the Future." A winning organisation thinks ahead and acts in good time, and future-focussed leadership is what sets apart the superior organisation from the mediocre one. This is discussed in greater detail in the next chapter.

What is important to note at this point is that to "Be in Time for the Future" offers strong motivation for continuous improvement and creative innovation. This call to action demands an organisation to be always questioning, always open to new ideas, and always willing to learn from anywhere. This requires a confident, courageous, and humble leadership that is able to engage in a debate over ideas without sinking into a battle of personalities.

LEADERSHIP EXCELLENCE. PEOPLE EXCELLENCE. POLICY EXCELLENCE. EXECUTION EXCELLENCE.

The outcome of attending carefully to Purpose, People, Principles, and Processes is to produce Organisational Excellence where organisations are at the best they can be.

As illustrated in The Circle of Excellence, there are four essential elements in this:

- **Leadership Excellence**
- **People Excellence**
- **Policy Excellence**
- **Execution Excellence**

EXCELLENCE DEVELOPMENT PROCESS

The sequencing is important.

- The essential starting point is **Leadership Excellence**: If Leadership is not directed towards excellence, none of the other aspects can happen.

- Next is **People Excellence**: Paying attention to helping everyone become and perform as best as they can is the key to superior organisational performance.

- Following that is **Policy Excellence**: Excellence in the thinking process of the company will yield superior plans, strategies, and policies.

- And finally, **Execution Excellence**: Excellence in the execution process manifests itself in superior performance, competitive positioning, and delighted customers. Shortcuts in driving just for performance will not build the foundations for sustained superior performance.

OUR GOAL MUST BE THE PROCESS

The Circle of Excellence applies just as well to the state, the corporation, the family, and the individual.

It is interesting that often for the family and the self, the focus is on capability and capacity-building, whereas for organisations the focus is just on the product and the service.

Why is it that when it comes to ourselves and our loved ones, we are principally concerned about what we can be as compared to what we already are, whereas when it comes to organisations, we are often principally concerned about the product and the service we do today? We must undo our thinking if we want our organisations to be excellent.

A happy client today does not assure a happy client tomorrow. Superior financial performance today does not assure sustained results tomorrow. Clear thinking, strong internal processes, a culture of continually honing skills and developing talent are what make organisations "future-ready."

Too often we think the goal is the product and the process is the means. The right way to think is that our goal must be the process: the

The Circle of Excellence applies just as well to the state, the corporation, the family, and the individual.

Too often we think the goal is the product and the process is the means.

Our goal must be the process.

The product as seen in today's performance is just the means to continually check how well the process is working out.

way we think, the way we execute, the way we build up capacity and capability, and the way we seek sustainable success. The product as seen in today's performance is just the means to continually check how well the process is working out.

CHALLENGE 9

KNOW WHERE YOU WANT TO GET TO

In the book *Alice's Adventures in Wonderland* by Lewis Carroll, we find Alice not sure which road she ought to take, when she sees a cat sitting on a nearby tree.

"Cheshire-Puss," she began, rather timidly, as she did not at all know whether it would like the name ... "Would you tell me, please, which way I ought to go from here?"

"That depends a good deal on where you want to get to," said the Cat.

"I don't much care where ..." said Alice.

"Then it doesn't matter which way you go," said the Cat.

"... so long as I get somewhere," Alice added as an explanation.

"Oh, you're sure to do that," said the Cat, "if you only walk long enough."

The story about Alice simply means that we ought to have an idea of what we want to achieve. Then we can plan what to do day by day.

This lesson applies not only to our work in the office, but also to our personal lives.

Achieving something worthwhile is not simply a matter of hoping to get somewhere. How we see things in life will determine how much we will accomplish.

I ask if you would imagine a stream with rocks in it.

The rocks stand firm. They do not move. They do not get anywhere.

The water makes its way continually past the rocks. Over a period of time, it will even wear the rocks down.

What would you compare your organisation to? Is it like the rocks, standing firm and steady, requiring the water to make its way around them? Or is it like the water, not held back by the rocks, but always working a way through?

The organisation should be life and movement — not unmoved and unmoving. We should never allow ourselves to be held back by barriers and obstacles. But at the same time we should stick with fundamental values such as honesty and integrity.

If we see ourselves as the rocks, we will not change. If we see ourselves as the water, we will not be held back.

The way of progress is change. We have to Learn. We have to Improve. We have to Innovate. This applies to the organisation. It also applies to us as individuals.

How do you see yourself in life? Do you have hopes of what you want to be and where you want to get to? Or are you like Alice, not really clear about your direction?

If we have our wishes for the future, do we see ourselves as able to change things for the better? Or are we unwilling to change or to try out new things?

If you see a problem, do you avoid it or do you try to do something about it? The Rock stands still. The Water in the stream will always find its way around. Do you see yourself as Rock or Water?

CHAPTER 9

The ultimate evidence of failed leadership is the failure of an organisation to meet the challenges of the ever-changing future and to sustain its success.

Mission comes before Vision.

Even as the Mission remains largely constant, the Vision has to be renewed from time to time if the organisation expects to survive and sustain success alongside changes in the environment.

Chapter 9

POSITION LEADERSHIP

As mentioned in the last chapter, Position Leadership requires us to be clear about the purpose and direction for our organisation or company. It expresses the Mission of the organisation and our Vision of what we would like it to become. It is working out the strategy for the organisation and what needs to be done to effectively execute the plans. It is defining the culture and the values that we believe are essential for sustained success for the company. It is, most of all, preparing and shaping the company for the future because, when all is said and done, the ultimate evidence of failed leadership is the failure of an organisation to meet the challenges of the ever-changing future and to sustain its success.

Mission comes before Vision. Mission defines the reason why the organisation exists, while Vision is the leader's expression of the tangible goals and outcomes that will define what success for the organisation is.

Even as the Mission remains largely constant, the Vision has to be renewed from time to time if the organisation expects to survive and sustain success alongside changes in the environment: customers' tastes and expectations change, as do income levels, competition, technology, and so on.

In order to bring one's organisation successfully into the future, the leader must manage the process of change well: if a leader fails in "future leadership" or "change leadership," he lets down the people in the organisation, even if he himself may have done well financially along the way.

The most common causes of the demise of successful organisations are the failure to:

- **Change in Good Times**
- **Change in Good Time**

LEADING FOR THE FUTURE

As previously mentioned, organisations suffer fatal failure for three reasons:

- A failure to learn from the past
- A failure to adapt to the present
- A failure to anticipate the future

Failure to learn from the past: The failure to learn from the past, either from past mistakes within the organisation itself or, even better, the mistakes of other organisations, is to ignore valuable lessons and learning opportunities!

Failure to adapt to the present: The failure to adapt to the present is the failure to recognise or admit that every policy or practice, when first adopted, is the best possible or practicable at that point, but as the external environment and customers change, the policies and practices become less and less relevant and more and more inappropriate for the time. The failure to adapt to the present is the surrender to bureaucracy or the triumph of indifference.

Failure to anticipate the future: The failure to change in good time and in good times is the triumph of complacency or the shortage of courage, and is probably the most common cause for the demise of successful organisations.

When things are going well for the organisation, costs are neglected and people who are not up to the job are kept on the pay-roll. However, when the business goes down, tough measures have to be taken in a hurry, and people may have to be retrenched when it is the worst of times for them.

An equally bad situation is when people who are adequate for the present but do not have adequate potential for higher degrees of responsibility are not helped or advised to seek a better place that can offer them better growth possibilities into the future. Thus, when a worker who is considered to be performing just satisfactorily is not advised to build his capability or advised to move elsewhere for a better job fit when

Responsible leadership has to be future-oriented and anticipative.

"We are moving from a world in which the big eat the small to a world in which the fast eat the slow."

Klaus Schwab

Amid all the future "unknowns," organisations need to have the capacity to plan ahead and anticipate the future, and at the same time have the ability to respond quickly to unexpected and unanticipated developments.

he is 30, and is later found to be unsatisfactory in his 40s and has to be asked to leave then, it would be a really bad event for him, for at that point he may well be bogged down with a mortgage or young children to see through university. Responsible leadership has to be future-oriented and anticipative.

The future is unknown, uncertain, and unpredictable. It is a future of increasing complexity with exploding information flow and an accelerating pace of change. As aptly expressed by Klaus Schwab, Founder of the World Economic Forum, "We are moving from a world in which the big eat the small to a world in which the fast eat the slow." Amid all these "unknowns," organisations need to have the capacity to plan ahead and anticipate the future as best they can, and at the same time have the ability to respond quickly to unexpected and unanticipated developments.

There are methods and approaches that can be used to address both these needs despite the lack of certainty. The former requires a disciplined way of thinking about the future, while the latter requires a disciplined way of reacting to events. While both are necessary, it is often difficult to find people who can do both well: the former often comprises the planners and strategists who want to see patterns and crave data and research to clarify their thinking, while the latter comprises operators and activists who are comfortable with ambiguity and uncertainty, and are prepared to act first before fully understanding. These two groups often see themselves as opposites, with feint respect for each other.

SCENARIO PLANNING

Scenario planning is a good way to anticipate an unknown and unknowable future. The book by Peter Schwartz entitled "The Art of the Long View — Planning for the Future in an Uncertain World" is an excellent reference and guide. Scenario planning delivers alternative views of the future by way of two, three, or four fundamentally different scenarios.

All the scenarios will be both plausible and possible. The methodology lies in identifying the driving forces that will have significant impact in shaping the future, differentiating the predetermined elements from

Scenario planning is a good way to anticipate an unknown and unknowable future.

Scenario planning draws out the:

- Known Knowns
- Known Unknowns
- Unknown Knowns

but not the Unknown Unknowns

Many of us are most comfortable with a Ready – Aim – Fire sequence of shooting, where time is available to get the weapon ready, to have a good aim at the target, and then to fire.

But responding to the unanticipated is often a matter of reversing the order to Fire – Aim – Ready.

the critical uncertainties. The biggest influencing factors are probably geography, demographics, and technology, as these often set the directions, or at least the boundaries, for politics and economics.

Scenario planning is certainly a good way of placing in an organised conceptual framework the "known knowns" about the future, the predetermined elements (like how the population is likely to grow), and also drawing out the "known unknowns" that are critical but cannot be known.

Scenario planning also brings out the "unknown knowns," these being the elements that can be known but may not have been given proper attention. But, practically by definition, scenario planning cannot deal with the "unknown unknowns"— these are what take organisations by surprise even though, on reflection, the organisation may later conclude that with more curiosity and imagination, and a greater dose of humility, the developments need not have been unanticipated.

Nevertheless, no matter how hard organisations may try to anticipate the future, there are always the blind spots and the sudden turns of event that surprise and shock. The resulting upheaval can even be fatal to organisations.

Reacting to the unexpected is an art and a frame of mind. If it is a repeat of, or similar to, some past event, then of course the appropriate department can be asked to handle it. But there are times when it is completely different, such as when the viral respiratory disease SARS (Severe Acute Respiratory Syndrome) first appeared in humans in late 2002. In such a scenario, a response is required even without adequate understanding of what the problem is — it is like dealing with a haemorrhage when the exact cause is not yet known, and the most critical action is to stop the haemorrhage before the patient succumbs to shock.

Many of us are most comfortable with a Ready – Aim – Fire sequence of shooting a gun, where time is available to get the weapon ready, to have a good aim at the target, and then to fire. But responding to the unanticipated is often a matter of reversing the order to Fire – Aim – Ready, where the most important first reaction is to fire, watch what gets knocked down to see if the bullets are getting to some sensible targets, after which the aim is constantly adjusted until the targets get knocked down.

The most critical skill a leader needs to have is the capacity to lead change.

Any organisation that strives for excellence must be an organisation that seeks change all the time as it seeks to be the best it can be.

Not everyone will be comfortable operating in this way, but it is necessary where failure is fatal and where patterns, understanding, theories, and systematic responses have not been developed.

CHANGE LEADERSHIP

As mentioned earlier, leadership is making things happen, which on their own would not happen. Therefore, the most critical skill a leader needs to have is the capacity to lead change. In this regard, anticipating the future and dealing with the unexpected is just one particular manifestation of change leadership.

Any organisation that strives for excellence must be an organisation that seeks change all the time as it seeks to be the best it can be. On the other hand, if change is going to happen without the leader being around, it is best that the leader not be around as he may be an unnecessary additional hurdle, whether real or perceived, in the change process.

CHANGE LEADERSHIP VS. CHANGE MANAGEMENT

Anyone who has tried to lead change knows that it is not a straightforward task. I use the term "change leadership" rather deliberately, distinguishing it from "change management."

By "change leadership," I mean a conscientious, persistent, and determined striving for change that will be good for the organisation, while by "change management," I refer to an approach involving the setting of plans and strategies, as well as lists and monitoring of goals and outcomes, but without that same discipline, insistence, and engagement that leadership demands.

CHANGE IN GOOD TIMES TO CHANGE IN GOOD TIME

It is exactly because change is often not easy to bring about that too many organisations begin the process of change only when faced with a crisis. When an organisation is in crisis, everybody expects something to be

It is always best to change in good times in order to change in good time.

To change without a crisis demands top management with foresight, insight, and a refined capacity for communication.

done, whether it be pleasant or otherwise, as long as it looks like action that at least somewhat addresses the problems. The need for change is obvious, and no one will be surprised by it; whether the change is welcome is a different matter.

However, there are two grave disadvantages when change is undertaken only when there is a crisis:

- An organisation in crisis is usually one in a state of low morale and high anxiety, especially given that people in an organisation often know that a crisis is looming before the public outside, or sometimes even the board of directors, know about it.

- Some of the best staff would have left the organisation, as they know things are in bad shape and reckon someplace else would be better able and willing to recognise their capabilities and welcome their contributions.

Dealing with an organisation of people with low morale and lesser capability unnecessarily adds to the challenges faced during the change process. Thus, it is always best to change in good times in order to change in good time.

There is also another critical advantage for changing when an organisation is not in crisis: should the staff have to leave or decide to leave, the best welfare they can be given is to leave when alternative jobs are much more easily available, and they have the time to seek such alternative jobs rather than have to leave in a hurry.

To change without a crisis demands top management with foresight, insight, and a refined capacity for communication. People need to see a need for change, so if the need is not obvious, unlike in a crisis, that need has to be effectively communicated so that people can understand the need and visualise the benefit of changing in good time.

BARRIERS TO CHANGE: PEOPLE BARRIERS AND RESOURCE BARRIERS

While the decision may be made to proceed with change, it does not mean that the process will be easy.

There are two sets of impediments to change:

- People Barriers
- Resource Barriers

People Barriers are often more difficult to overcome because of issues of anxiety, mistrust, incompetence, and non-cooperation.

Resource Barriers are easier to overcome, either by allocation of funds or creative use of available resources, or both.

There are two sets of impediments to change:

- People Barriers
- Resource Barriers

Between the two, People Barriers are often more difficult to deal with because issues of anxiety, mistrust, incompetence, and non-cooperation need to be overcome. The Resource Barriers are easier to overcome, either by allocation of funds or creative use of available resources, or both.

For the change process to succeed, ways have to be found to remove the barriers, to go over them, or to go around them. This requires imagination and determination, the forcefulness of will, and often more critically, the empathy of heart. Leaders have to recognise that change is an issue of hearts and minds, not simply an issue of clear intentions and detailed plans.

PEOPLE BARRIERS

There are four kinds of People Barriers:

- Beliefs Barrier
- Knowledge Barrier
- Confidence Barrier
- Power Barrier

Beliefs Barrier: The Beliefs Barrier is where people do not support a change because they perceive it as going against the values and beliefs they have about what the organisation is for and how the organisation should go about its business.

In other words, they feel that the proposed change will undermine the purpose or the character of the organisation as they understand it. They have to be brought around to at least recognise a case for the proposed change, even if they may not instinctively or emotionally accept it, by being convinced that the change does not undermine the mission of the organisation, but is an attempt to keep the organisation

There are four kinds of People Barriers:

- **Beliefs Barrier**
- **Knowledge Barrier**
- **Confidence Barrier**
- **Power Barrier**

up-to-date and relevant under changing circumstances, resulting from changes in demographics, technology and/or the cultural or social environment.

Knowledge Barrier: The Knowledge Barrier is where people do not support a change because, based on their knowledge and experience, they either do not see the necessity to change or the wisdom of changing in the way envisaged by their leadership.

People who raise the Knowledge Barrier have to be brought around by helping them see that there are good and strong reasons to change. This may be done by showing them facts and data, or having them visit competitor or peer organisations, or bringing them to the operating level to see for themselves that the identified problems are real and there is clear imperative to change. People who pose the Knowledge Barrier are basically objective and rational, and they can be won over by facts and reason.

Confidence Barrier: The Confidence Barrier is where people do not support a change because they do not have the confidence and conviction that the effort to change will be successful, and therefore prefer not to attempt the change. The reason why they do not think the effort to change will work may be varied — for example, they may perceive that senior management is only paying lip service or is not fully committed, and therefore will not have the stamina or give the necessary time and resources for the effort to succeed. Alternatively, they may not think their colleagues will give genuine attention or support for the change, or they may believe that the change will be too complex to be able to maintain the interest and attention of those affected for long enough.

The people who raise the Confidence Barrier are not against the outcomes hoped for — they simply do not think the hopes would be realised, and they are uncomfortable with ambiguity and the uncertainty of success. They need to have their confidence to handle the proposed change built up by providing them with thorough training and involving them in the design of the change process, as well as strengthened by way of encouragement and explicit support of senior management.

Resource Barriers may be due to the lack of:

- **Time and attention from senior management**
- **Budget for capital expenditure**
- **Equipment and expertise**

Resource Barriers have to be addressed by way of persuasion, negotiation, and even "barter trading."

There is nothing like small successes that give credibility to requests for more resources to build upon the success.

Power Barrier: The Power Barrier is where people do not support a change because it would undermine their power and authority. This can be a particularly difficult barrier to identify because the people who are putting up the Power Barrier can hardly ever be expected to proclaim that they are objecting because the change would undermine their position and standing in the organisation. Instead, they will offer reasons that make them sound, more honourably, as being caught by the Beliefs Barrier, or the Knowledge Barrier, or the Confidence Barrier, when in fact the problem is the Power Barrier. While every attempt should be made to bring them on board the change process by, for example, making them a sponsor of the change process, it has to be recognised that in many instances they will refuse to come on board.

RESOURCE BARRIERS

Resource Barriers exist when people believe that the resources will not be forthcoming to effectively execute the change and they therefore prefer not to start. Resource Barriers are, however, much easier to address once the People Barriers are adequately addressed.

The Resource Barriers may be due to the lack of:

- Time and attention from senior management
- Budget for capital expenditure
- Equipment and expertise, which may be under the control of other departments or agencies.

Resource Barriers have to be addressed by way of persuasion, negotiation, and even "barter trading." One common mistake is to ask for too much too early. There is nothing like small successes that give credibility to requests for more resources to build upon the success, so conduct experiments with the resources at hand to demonstrate the worthiness of investing in the new idea, and only then ask for more resources.

TO DEFER OR PRESS ON?

The Circle of Improvement, illustrates why change efforts commonly fail, and why it is a leader's responsibility to bring his or her people from a

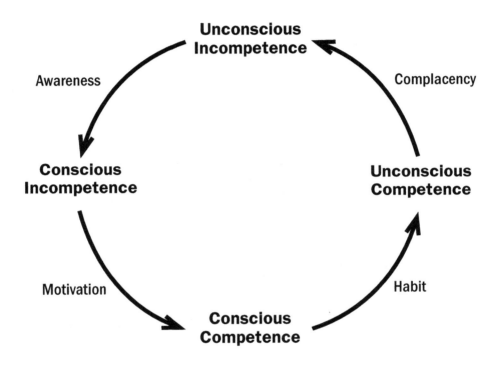

THE CIRCLE OF IMPROVEMENT

state of unconscious incompetence to a state of unconscious competence.

Unconscious Incompetence: Many organisations start in a state of "unconscious incompetence," as the entire organisation or parts of the organisation are unaware of their inadequacies.

Conscious Incompetence: There comes a day when management becomes aware of the organisation's inadequacies and brings the organisation into a state of "conscious incompetence." This awareness may arise through peer comparison, visiting other organisations, reading literature, etc.

Conscious Competence: If there is the desire to improve, the organisation will conduct studies, send its staff for training programmes, review its processes, and so on; as a result, the organisation will enter into a state of "conscious competence." Almost invariably, what happens at this point is that someone will produce a series of work rules, or standard operating procedures, for others to follow. These rules are particularly useful for new comers who now have a step by step guide to doing a good job, without necessarily understanding the reasons for the rules.

Unconscious Competence: When the people in the organisation do not understand why they are doing what they are doing, the organisation enters into a state of "unconscious competence," where its customers, at least for a time, will still reckon they are getting good service despite the service provider not fully knowing why it is competent.

The state of "unconscious competence" is the danger zone, because, being "unconscious," the organisation will, sooner or later, slip into a state of "unconscious incompetence" without knowing how or when it got there.

This transition into incompetence almost invariably happens because the environment has changed — customers' needs have become different, consumers have changed, competitors have entered the market, technology has brought in new methods and new expectations, and so on.

Organisations that do not continually question what they are

Organisations that do not continually question what they are doing and how they are doing it run the danger of being caught in "unconsciousness."

There are times when objections on account of the Power Barrier, and sometimes also the Beliefs Barrier, simply cannot be reasoned off or overcome.

In these instances, the people who are objecting may have to be asked to step aside, suspend their judgment, and allow the change to proceed.

Change is difficult, even dangerous, but change is the very essence of the function of leadership.

doing and how they are doing it run the danger of being caught in "unconsciousness," and the resulting complacency may well be fatal for the organisation.

Very often when people raise objections to a change, the tendency is to deal with every reluctance as though it were a case of the Knowledge Barrier, and therefore more reasoning would help. If the organisational response to communicate and explain more does not work, the organisation must seriously think of pushing on with the change nonetheless.

While there will be occasions when deferring a change proposal and waiting for a more opportune time would be the wisest thing to do, there are also times when this would not be the most appropriate response.

The fact is that not all objections are on account of the Knowledge Barrier. There are times when objection on account of the Power Barrier, and sometimes also the Beliefs Barrier, simply cannot be reasoned off or overcome. In these instances, the people who are objecting may have to be asked to step aside, suspend their judgment, and allow the change to proceed; not proceeding with the change may simply be the wrong thing to do, and may even be fatal for the organisation.

Never forget that there is no change without disagreement. Machiavelli once remarked: "It must be considered that there is nothing more difficult to carry out, nor more dangerous to handle, than to initiate a new order of things. For the reformer has enemies in all those who profit by the old order, and only lukewarm defenders in all those who would profit by the new order."

It would not be unusual for organisations to reach a point where the situation has to be starkly put across to their people: "The train is about to leave the station. You have the choice to get on the train or to get off the train, but don't get in front of the train."

So change is difficult, even dangerous, but change is the very essence of the function of leadership, for which the failure to change may simply be catastrophic for the organisation.

IN CLOSING…

I have outlined what people expect of their leaders in their positions. Leaders can get the desired responses from their people by threat or

"It must be considered that there is nothing more difficult to carry out, nor more dangerous to handle, than to initiate a new order of things. For the reformer has enemies in all those who profit by the old order, and only lukewarm defenders in all those who would profit by the new order."

Machiavelli

persuasion; the approach will make an enormous difference to how much their people will commit their minds and hearts to achieve the desired outcomes. People may be doing just enough to satisfy their bosses by doing just what they are told — this is like hiring brains and hands and feet, without winning hearts and minds. And when people do not give all of themselves in their work, the organisation fails to reach its highest potential. Pulling at the hearts is the result of superior Personal Leadership, which I will cover in the next chapter.

CHALLENGE 10

CHOOSE TO SEE THE BEST IN OTHERS

Tommy simply cannot sit still in kindergarten. During storytelling time, he talks and walks about. He disturbs other children in their work. Instead of taking a nap, he runs around the room. The teacher cannot control him, and thinks he is a real troublemaker.

On Teachers' Day, the children gave little presents to their teacher. Tommy also had a present for her. It was a little box, wrapped with pretty coloured paper. She opened the box slowly and carefully. Inside was a caterpillar. The teacher thought it was a naughty trick. She became very angry and scolded Tommy. She threw the box into the wastepaper basket.

After school, the teacher found a little envelope. It must have dropped from one of the presents. Inside was a letter for her, from Tommy. The letter said, "Dear Teacher, here is a baby butterfly for you. I hope it will become a pretty butterfly."

The teacher felt very bad. Tommy had wanted to do a good thing. But she had thrown away his gift and scolded him. Why? It was because she thought Tommy was naughty, and everything he did must be naughty.

Often, many of us are actually like the teacher.

For example, if someone has done something wrong one day, we think he will never be able to do anything right. No matter what he does later on, we don't care to look at it because we think it cannot be good.

Another example: If we see someone unable to walk normally because he had suffered from polio when he was young, we also think his brain may not be normal, so we do not include him in discussions, and we do not give him tough jobs. And then we wonder why his work is not very good.

You can call this "prejudice." You can call this "assumptions." Others call it "mental models." It means the way we think about people prevents us from seeing how capable they are or from understanding them well.

A third example: If we believe our customers want to cheat us, we will make all kinds of rules to control them. But if we believe most of our customers are honest and law-abiding, we will make things convenient for them, and at the same time think of ways to catch the few who may want to cheat. In this way, we do not allow the small number of bad customers to cause us to delay our service to all the other customers.

Let us be willing to question our "mental models," whether these "mental models" apply to our customers, our colleagues, or our work. Let us not allow our "mental models" to prevent us from seeing possibilities and taking up opportunities for offering better service or producing better results. This is the way to get an excellent public service — always questioning, always improving, always willing to do better.

Our "mental models" must allow us to see the future beautiful butterfly, and not just the ugly hairy caterpillar.

CHAPTER 10

The Essence of Leadership:

- **Not Position but Followers**
- **Not Popularity but Results**
- **Not Preaching but Examples**
- **Not Privileges but Responsibility**

Chapter 10

PERSONAL LEADERSHIP

Personal Leadership is what makes Position Leadership succeed the best way possible. It is a matter of engaging both the hearts and minds of our people. It makes people want to follow you because they sense that there is something worthy about your abilities, something sincere about your concern, and something inspiring about your example that moves them to be the best they can be, and to aspire to be a leader themselves.

If we do not have followers, we are not a leader. This is such an obvious definition but is one that is often missed. We may be called Chairman or CEO or Director or Commander, but we are not a leader if we do not have willing followers.

As succinctly expressed by Peter F. Drucker in "The Leader of the Future," the essence of leadership is:

- Not Position but Followers
- Not Popularity but Results
- Not Preaching but Examples
- Not Privileges but Responsibility

This is not to say that a good leader has to be a soft-hearted, affable, gregarious, and jovial person who never wields the stick, and leaves his or her people to do as much as they want of whatever they wish to do. People will often follow leaders who are very tough and demanding, but with a quality about them that make them worthy of followership. Those who have been in the military, for example, know that those among their army mates whom they would like as their friends are often not the same people as those they would like to have as their leaders in battle!

Every person is made up of:

- **Body**
- **Soul**
- **Spirit**

The effective leader has to recognise one's ideal as connecting with the spirit of the people to motivate them to seek and do what they know to be the best and correct thing.

One thing is certain: The follower believes he is better off having the person as his leader - whether it be out of fear for his livelihood or his well-being, or out of respect for what the leader is doing for the follower's life. If followership is the critical factor in leadership, it is obviously necessary to understand leadership from the perspective of the prospective follower.

What I am assuming here is that we desire to unlock the total capability of our people, and are not simply satisfied with getting one task or another done.

Getting the immediate job done can very much be just a matter of training, direction, and perhaps threat — but getting the job done with pride, with attention to detail, with cheerful delivery, with an eye always on quality and reliability, with a desire for continual improvement, and with a passion to constantly innovate, requires the total harnessing of the hearts and minds of our people.

It is useful here to speak a little bit more about the make-up of people. Every person is made up of three parts:

- Body
- Soul
- Spirit

Body: The body is that part of us which comprises our five senses connecting us to the world around us — the sense of sight, of hearing, of smell, of taste, and of touch. We see what others do, we hear what they say, we look for the aroma and taste in what we eat, and so on. The body is what gives us "world consciousness."

Soul: The soul can be said to have three aspects — the intellect (what we think), the emotion (what we feel), and the will (our power to decide).

We each have the power to decide either rationally, using our minds, or emotionally, using our hearts, or usually some combination of the two. The way we decide may simply be to follow what others do, in which case we are allowing those elements of our senses that connect with what we see and hear around us to determine our course forward.

Alternatively, we may decide based on some inner compass in our beings, based on values and the sense of morals and ethics we each hold,

The **GEESE** Leadership Framework high-
lights the five essential things people want
their leaders to do:

- **G**uide
- **E**mpathise
- **E**nergise
- **S**ynergise
- **E**mbolden

which enters into the realm of the third part of human beings, the spirit. The soul is what gives us "self-consciousness." It is what makes each one of us different from others in the way we think and feel and act.

Spirit: The spirit is our innermost being. One of the most important aspects of the spirit is the conscience. The conscience is our "built-in compass" that gives us our sense of what is good or bad in thought and behaviour, as well as what is right or wrong in our action. The spirit is what gives us "god-consciousness."

Even though we may not all agree exactly on what is good and bad, or what is right and wrong, the point simply is that each of us has this inner compass. Our thoughts and feelings and subsequently our decisions — in other words, the functioning of our souls — may be driven by what we see happening in the world around us (i.e. the elements of our body), or may be driven by what we believe in our inner self (i.e. our spirit).

The reason for going into this short discourse about body, soul, and spirit, is that the effective leader has to see his task as not simply giving directives and demanding compliance (which is operating on the "body" aspects of his people) but has to recognise his ideal as connecting with the spirit of the people to motivate them to seek and do what they know to be the best and correct thing. Hence, if supervisors expect full engagement and full realisation of the potential of the organisation, they need to "release" their people to be the best they can be.

GEESE LEADERSHIP FRAMEWORK

A few years back, a team of staff volunteered to do a study for me on the qualities people look for in their supervisors. Their conclusion was immensely interesting. There are just five essential things people want their supervisors to do, and these can be easily remembered with the acronym **GEESE**.

- **G**uide
- **E**mpathise

The leader who is able to guide, and guide well, is one who is open to learning continually so as to constantly be up-to-date.

Leaders must be really interested in the well-being of their people, be willing to listen to their feedback, and to understand their needs and motivations by looking at things from their perspective.

Empathising with your people means to walk with them, and if you expect them to run, then to run with them.

- **E**nergise
- **S**ynergise
- **E**mbolden

GUIDE

Supervisors must be knowledgeable and capable, and at the same time have the desire to "show the way" by counselling and training their people so that they may do their job as best as possible.

Competence is the first thing followers look for in their bosses. The worst kind of boss is the one who tells you to get something done but has no idea himself how it should or can be done; this is not to say that bosses need to know everything, let alone know everything in every detail, but they must be capable or knowledgeable of something that their followers find useful and important for getting the job done. In a world where knowledge is increasing at an explosive rate, the leader who is able to guide, and guide well, is one who is open to learning continually so as to constantly be up-to-date.

EMPATHISE

To empathise means to be able to feel for and with another person, so supervisors must be really interested in the well-being of their people, be willing to listen to their feedback, and to understand their needs and motivations by looking at things from their perspective.

Empathising with your people means to walk with them, and if you expect them to run, then to run with them. It has been said that you cannot expect your people to care about their work if they do not believe that you care about them, so the starting point to having your people put in their best and contribute their most must be their sensing that you are concerned about their well-being and that you want them to succeed.

A very powerful application of empathy is for each of us to continually ask the question: "How can I help you do your job better?"

Indeed, if leaders would remember nothing else about what would most likely make people want to follow them, they should remember

A very powerful application of empathy is for each of us to continually ask the question: "How can I help 'you' do your job better?"

"You" refers to:

- Your boss
- Your peers
- Your subordinates
- Yourself

In order to energise one's staff, leaders must somehow be able to have their people engaged and interested in their work

this question, because the question expresses personal interest and the willingness to help others.

Who does the "you" refer to?

First and foremost, "you" refers to your own boss. Always try to help your boss succeed and never try to undermine his position or help him to fail (though if he chooses not to have your help and drives himself into trouble, there is nothing you can do). The reason you want your boss to be clear that you are always willing to do what you can to help him succeed is to thereby gain his trust and boost your credibility — he is then much more likely to grant you the freedom to decide and act. You will receive the "empowerment" so many people crave for but do not get because they have not established a state of trust with their bosses.

The next "you" refers to your peers. I know this may sound odd because too many people regard their peers as competitors rather than helpmates. But in today's world of complexity, there are very few instances where we can get a proposal through or a job done all on our own, so having the goodwill of your peers is an excellent proposition. If they will not go out of the way to help you, they will at least be unlikely to go out of the way to get you into trouble.

The next "you" refers, obviously, to the people who report to you. Nothing will boost their willingness to follow you more than them knowing that you are prepared to help them succeed. You need to have the heart for them. Bear in mind they will very easily read you if you are not sincere about it. Your authentic self must be a self that cares.

There is a final "you" that perhaps should even be the first "you." I am referring to yourself. What are you doing to help yourself? Are you continuously learning and wanting to do better and pushing yourself to excellence and doing all this with a conviction and purposefulness that shows up in your face and your body language?

ENERGISE

In order to energise one's staff, leaders must somehow be able to have their people engaged and interested in their work. There is no way supervisors can have people who are full of energy and drive if they are not keen about their work. The most critical requirement is that leaders themselves must

Leaders themselves must be energised.

There are four different kinds of energy:
- **Physical energy**
- **Mental energy**
- **Emotional energy**
- **Spiritual energy**

be energised. It is not difficult at all to sense whether people are energised about their work — it will show in their faces and attitude towards their work. When people are not energised at work, almost invariably we will find that their immediate bosses are not energised, though the opposite may not hold, as energised supervisors may not necessarily result in energised staff.

There are four kinds of energy: physical energy, mental energy, emotional energy, and spiritual energy.

- **Physical energy** refers to the physical fitness of the individual. It is the basic source of fuel in one's life. If we are not physically fit, it will affect our mental energy and emotional energy, if not also our spiritual energy. Think of the times we are sick even if it were just a cough and slight fever — it immediately impacts our sense of well-being, reduces our capacity to concentrate, and perhaps gives us a shortness of temper, if not simply an unwillingness to interact with others.

- **Emotional Energy**: Jim Loehr and Tony Schwartz posit in their book, "The Power of Full Engagement," that in order to perform at our best, we must access pleasant and positive emotions to experience enjoyment, challenge, adventure, and opportunity.

- **Mental Energy** is what we use to organise our lives and focus our attention, and reflect our capacity to withstand mental pressures and emotional strains.

- **Spiritual energy** provides the force for action in all dimensions of our lives and derives its strength from the depths of a person's being — deeply held values and a purpose beyond one's self-interest. It may be a legacy one wants to leave behind, a to-do list of what one wants to accomplish in life, or it may be a drive to please the god of one's beliefs. The courage and conviction to live by our deepest values, supported by passion, commitment, integrity, and honesty are the key muscles that fire spiritual energy. As spiritual energy may grip a person's mind, heart and fuel his passion in life,

The energy level of people is very much affected by their philosophy of life as well as the energy level of their bosses.

In order to synergise successfully, the supervisor must be able to:

- Persuade and communicate well in order to manage relationships
- Traverse organisational boundaries
- Ensure that there is sufficient diversity in the system
- Leverage on subordinates' diverse talents to ensure a holistic approach to issues

spiritual energy can directly impact a person's mental energy and emotional energy, even more than his physical energy.

This whole discussion of energy levels is important, because the energy level of people — the passion they bring to work and life — is very much affected by their philosophy of life, as well as the energy level of their bosses.

Since energy is one of those things that is caught, rather than taught, energy levels cannot simply be directed or prescribed by supervisors; more often than not, they are heavily influenced by the drive and passion of the supervisors themselves who may create a work environment that bubbles with energy or who burst whatever bubbles of energy there may be.

SYNERGISE

It is important to synergise an organisation to help people and departments work together so that the result of their work is more than what they can accomplish if each person or department works on its own.

In order to synergise successfully, the supervisor must be able to persuade and communicate well in order to manage relationships, traverse organisational boundaries, ensure that there is sufficient diversity in the system, and leverage on subordinates' diverse talents to ensure a holistic approach to issues.

Too often supervisors take the easy way out: they tell their staff to get the job done, and to settle any problems at the working level; however, many a time, the issues simply cannot be settled at the working level. Sometimes the problem is the unwillingness on the part of colleagues in other departments to cooperate, but oftentimes, synergies cannot be attained because each department has its own agenda, its own set of priorities, and its own concerns.

The only way to overcome the problem is for the supervisors of the respective departments to speak with each other and align their agendas, then only can their respective staff move on to get the job done when they have been given the official clearance by their bosses to help each other.

This task of clearing obstacles and paving the way is often neglected,

If you want an organisation that is innovative, creative, and is always looking out for ways to improve and be better, you need people who have the courage to challenge the *status quo*, and try out new things and new ways of doing things.

ignored, or simply avoided by supervisors, because they wish to be "nice" to each other and to "keep the peace," yet supervisors expect their subordinates below them to get the job done. It is an intense source of frustration for many people at the working level, and results in the perception that their supervisors are irresponsible, unthinking, unreasonable, uncaring, and spineless.

EMBOLDEN

To Embolden means that supervisors give their people the courage to try new things, and to speak out when they are unclear or disagree — this will only happen if supervisors create work environments in which it is safe to offer different ideas, to innovate, and to make mistakes and learn from them.

If you want an organisation that is innovative, creative, and is always looking out for ways to improve and be better, you need people who have the courage to challenge the *status quo*, and try out new things and new ways of doing things.

An organisation bubbling with energy needs courage to support ideas, conduct experiments, and learn from mistakes. However, oftentimes, change does not happen because bosses have "no brains, no heart, or no guts":

- "No brains" in the sense that they are not able or willing to consider an idea if success were not assured, even if the idea is at least worthy of being tried out.

- "No heart" in the sense that they do not care about the feelings of their subordinates and others, and are only concerned about meeting their own targets, no matter how they are achieved.

- "No guts" in the sense that they do not have the courage to try out new ideas or to give their people permission to try out the ideas because they are scared of the responsibility and accountability.

"It is better to ask for forgiveness than permission": if you are prepared to take responsibility for your thoughts and actions, you should be prepared to act on your convictions.

Embolden your people and freely forgive their good intentions, but at the same time, also insist on rigorous learning and be firm that any mistakes from the past should never be repeated.

FORGIVENESS

While emboldening the staff is critical for high-performing organisations, there is also the critical need to have the ability to forgive.

There is an adage: "It is better to ask for forgiveness than permission." When you seek the permission of your boss to do something, you are passing to him accountability and responsibility for your actions, because, if things should fail, he had given you the permission to proceed.

In many new and novel situations, bosses cannot be faulted for being extra cautious, and the easiest decision they can give is "No." Once they say "No," it is the end of your hope to think or do differently. However, if you are prepared to take responsibility for your thoughts and actions, you should be prepared to act on your convictions and, if things should go wrong, seek your boss' forgiveness.

It is easier for a supervisor to forgive, as forgiveness stems from an assessment of character — "Was my subordinate acting honestly and in good faith?" — whereas permission requires an assessment of the proposal and the assumption of responsibility.

So embolden your people, and freely forgive their good intentions, but at the same time, also insist on rigorous learning and be firm that any mistakes from the past should never be repeated.

IN CLOSING...

The ideas in the GEESE Leadership Framework are simple, but, as with all things, the adoption and execution is perhaps not so easy.

Personal leadership is first and foremost a matter of the heart. The GEESE Leadership Framework requires a leader to have the desire to help his or her people be the best they can be, so they can contribute the most to the organisation, both individually and collectively.

CHALLENGE 11

EMPATHISE WITH OTHERS

The little girl was late in coming home. Her mother had sent her to the shop to buy something. She should have been back half an hour ago.

The door opened and in came the girl. Her mother asked, "Where have you been? You should have been back 30 minutes ago."

"Sorry, Mother," she said. "As I was coming back, I saw Lucy next door. She was crying. Her doll was broken. So I stopped to help her."

Her mother was very puzzled. How could her little girl help Lucy with a broken doll?

"What did you do to help her?"

"I sat down next to her, and cried with her," the little girl said.

We can learn at least three things from this story.

First, when someone is late or does not get a job done, do not simply start shouting and scolding the person. Ask him for the reason. Give him a chance to explain. Ask questions. Things may not be what you imagine. Don't jump to conclusions. Be willing to understand.

Second, always be willing to help someone else in whatever way you can. It will give you a new dose of happiness. Happiness is something you can give to someone else, and at the same time you still have it after you give it away.

The third point is the most important of all. We can always help. It is not a matter of money. It is not a matter of skills. It is a matter of willingness. It is our attitude towards other people. It is a matter of the heart, not just of the mind.

Think of the little girl. Did she help Lucy? In fact, she did not do anything to repair the doll. The doll was still broken. But she did something much more valuable. She showed her friend she really cared. When her friend was sad, she was sad also. So she helped her friend by being there for her when she cried.

Show that you care for your parents, your children, your friends, your office colleagues, and those around you. Help them solve their problems if you can. But if you can't do anything to solve their problems, show that you care about their feelings.

If people are happy, be happy with them. If they are sad, be sad with them. People call this showing empathy for others. "Empathy" is too big a word. Keep it simple. Show others you care for them. Help them in whatever way you can, even if it is no more than joining them in their weeping.

CONCLUDING THOUGHTS

Sometimes the shepherd breaks the leg of the lamb in order to teach it a lesson it will not easily forget!

Shepherds have to exercise "tough love" to discipline their sheep — this is as much their role as is being a protector, and fending off predators and thieves.

If any sheep should stray from the flock and get lost, the shepherd will exercise every effort to find the sheep and celebrate the rescue each time it happens.

THE
LEADER
THE
TEACHER

I have been asked what I would liken the leader to. One good model would be the shepherd.

THE SHEPHERD LEADER

The shepherd serves as a guide, provider, and protector. Sheep know exactly who their shepherd is and follow their shepherd. More importantly, the shepherd knows his sheep; he guides them to pasture and to water, and protects his flock from thieves and predators.

When thinking of shepherding, we often visualise the romantic picture of a shepherd with a lamb across his shoulder and think that his favourite sheep gets the privilege to be carried around. What often eludes us is that, more than likely, the lamb is being carried around because it has a broken leg — a leg broken by the shepherd himself!

There are dangerous places a sheep should not go to. If a sheep gets into trouble, the shepherd uses his staff — the cane with a hook at the end — to get the sheep out of danger: he puts the hook around the leg of the sheep and pulls it out.

There are, however, lambs that do not learn fast or learn well, and they keep getting into dangerous situations. So sometimes the shepherd breaks the leg of the lamb in order to teach it a lesson it will not easily forget! Shepherds have to exercise "tough love" to discipline their sheep; this is as much their role as is being a protector, and fending off predators and thieves. And you can be sure that if any sheep should stray from the

The test of great leadership is not only that good things happen and many things get done while the leader is around; the true test is the legacy that a leader leaves for the sustained and continual success, progress, and development of the organisation.

A leader's most critical contributions are what still remains when the leader is no longer around!

Not everyone has the same innate capabilities but each of us can be a leader in our own sphere, at our own level, and in our own right.

flock and get lost, the shepherd will exercise every effort to find the sheep and celebrate the rescue each time it happens.

There is a very real parallel between a shepherd and a good leader, in terms of the requisite care, guidance, provision, and protection — so many bosses fail even at this level! But this is only the base level for good leadership.

What should the best leader be doing? A great leader should be making good things happen, which on their own would not happen, and he or she will, in the great majority of cases, have to accomplish this through people: bosses, peers, and most of all, subordinates.

The test of great leadership is not only that good things happen and many things get done while the leader is around; the true test is the legacy that a leader leaves for the sustained and continual success, progress, and development of the organisation. In short, a leader's most critical contributions are what still remains when the leader is no longer around.

This is not to say that successful performance while the leader is in charge is not important: ongoing success is always important, but great success is to be judged by what endures in the thinking, values, and beliefs of the organisation and its staff, even if the practices have to change with time and circumstances.

Every one of us likes to succeed, and all of us like to feel good about ourselves. There is nothing more motivating than to discover that we are able to do things well and to stretch ourselves beyond our perceived limits to reach our potential. Indeed, life becomes exciting and energising when each new accomplishment becomes evidence that we can do more than we had imagined possible, and we realise that we have limited ourselves in what we imagine we were capable of.

We seek bosses that allow us to learn, stretch, and discover ourselves. We seek leaders who seek to make us leaders. Not everyone has the same innate capabilities but each of us can be a leader in our own sphere, at our own level, and in our own right.

Very often when things need to get done and people are somewhat sceptical about whether they would get done, they often cite that what is required is "buy-in by top management" and "leadership by example." Most times when they say this, they are in fact softly voicing criticism of the current leadership. But more than that, they wish for a chance, in due course, to be leaders themselves.

LEADERSHIP DEVELOPMENT PROCESS

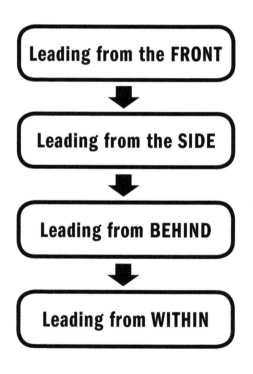

FOUR STAGES IN LEADERSHIP DEVELOPMENT PROCESS

An interesting question is where the leader should be leading relative to his people. I posit four stages in the leadership development process:

- **Leading from the Front**
- **Leading from the Side**
- **Leading from Behind**
- **Leading from Within**

Leading from the Front is where most people expect their leaders to be. When anyone is first assigned a new appointment, it is essential that the leader leads from the front to demonstrate competence, willingness to do whatever he or she is asking his or her people to do, ability to guide, capacity for empathy, as well as commitment and passion for the job. It is only natural for the people in an organisation to "test out" new leaders before they commit their followership to them.

However, leading from the front is only a starting position. It will not generate the next level of leadership, and is not what their people fundamentally wish for. What people want is to taste success for themselves, and realise their potential.

Leading from the Side: Once the leader has earned trust and credibility with his people, he has to consider moving from "leading from the front" to "leading from the side" to serve as the pacesetter and the standard bearer. This means helping his people get things done, and giving them the opportunity to try and to learn so as to discover what they are capable of, and more importantly, to taste the sweetness of success for themselves.

By insisting that your people learn to do things themselves, and always being there for them to provide help, guidance, support, and protection so that they are able to perform with confidence, the leader builds the self-esteem and self-confidence of the next generation of leaders.

Leading from Behind: After leading from the side, the leader should next move to "leading from behind." This formulation of leadership might

The ultimate goal for any leader is to "lead from within."

This means that the leader has so successfully implanted and generated values, capability, capacity, confidence, attitudes, and ways of thinking and competence that the leader has developed the next generation of leaders that would be best able to lead the organisation for the future.

sound strange but is actually an essential step to building confidence and generating the next leadership.

When you lead from behind, your people are left to get on with the task, discover things for themselves, and even make mistakes along the way; but you are constantly there to monitor what they are doing and to bring to their attention potential pitfalls and new challenges that might surprise your staff. Rather than providing step-by-step directions to his or her people, the leader helps them discover the way forward and, in the process, grow as individuals and as future leaders because they are energised by the challenges, but are never allowed to be overwhelmed by them.

Leading from Within: Leading from the front, then moving to leading from the side, and then leading from behind are the stages involved in establishing oneself as a worthy leader and growing the next generation, but the ultimate goal in generating leaders is to be "leading from within." This means that the leader has so successfully implanted values and generated capability, capacity, confidence, attitudes, and ways of thinking that the leader has developed the next generation of leaders that would be best able to lead the organisation in the future.

This process of leading from the front, to leading from the side, to leading from behind, to leading from within, can perhaps be more simply visualised as the process of moving from "I do, you watch" to "We do" to "You do, I watch" to "You do." It is the ultimate gift the leader can offer his people. Seen in this way, the leader as shepherd is a valid but inadequate model. I think the much more appropriate model is the leader as teacher.

THE LEADER, THE TEACHER

As mentioned in Chapter Four, there is something very special about teaching, which makes the profession distinctly different from any other.

The most critical difference between teaching and working virtually anywhere else is this: The more the student surpasses his or her teacher, the greater the success of the teacher, whereas in the office, the higher

The idea of success itself is totally different for a teacher — it is a definition that is focussed on the success of others, not the success of one's self.

If a leader sees his or her role not just to lead well for today but to build well for the future, his or her best contribution then is as a teacher *par excellence*, whose concern is first and foremost the success of his or her people.

the position a person gets to in the organisation, the more successful he or she is deemed to be — so we need not be surprised with bosses who work hard at keeping their people down.

The idea of success itself is totally different for a teacher. It is a definition that is focussed on the success of others, not the success of one's self. I applaud everyone who has dedicated his or her life to be a teacher, for whom teaching is not a job or an occupation, but an honourable vocation and a high calling.

Teaching is an enormous privilege, a great responsibility, and an unparalleled opportunity to do good for the lives of others. I am always inspired when the teacher does not say I teach science or mathematics or literature, but simply says, "I teach children."

"Moulding the future of our nation" is not an empty slogan of the Ministry of Education — it truly reflects the power in the hands of the teacher to make or break lives.

If a leader sees his role as not just to lead well for today but to build well for the future, his best contribution then is as a teacher: identifying potential, recognising effort, encouraging ideas, and pursuing excellence with a continuous drive for the organisation to be the best it can be and the people to be the best they can be. A leader's best role is therefore to be a teacher *par excellence*, whose concern is first and foremost the success of his or her people.

I have chronicled what I have learnt and conceived about leadership over more than three decades heading a variety of institutions, mostly in the Singapore public sector.

As the focus of the ideas presented in this book are on people, I am convinced that the thoughts and practices I have outlined would apply equally to the private sector and the people sector (also referred to in other literature as "the third sector"), and contain applicable truths for individuals and families.

Throughout my various appointments, I have found people to be much the same everywhere: they want to succeed, they want to feel good about themselves, they want to be self-confident, and they want to contribute towards the performance and development of their organisation. They seek leadership that is forward-looking, competent, empathetic, energising, courageous, and above all, focussed on

"太上，不知有之；

其次，亲而誉之；

其次，畏之；

其次，侮之；

信不足焉，有不信焉。

悠兮其贵言。

功成、事遂，

百姓皆谓：我自然。"

"As for the best leaders,
the people do not notice their existence.
The next best,
the people honour and praise.
The next, the people fear;
and the next, the people hate.
When the best leader's work is done,
his aim fulfilled,
the people will say,
'We did it ourselves!'"

Laozi

developing their people to be the best that they can possibly be, and to enable them to go as far they possibly can.

The real question is: "Where is such selflessness in the leader to come from?" Well, it really goes deep into our inner motivations as leadership is ultimately a matter of the heart.

Laozi (老子), the ancient Chinese philosopher, cast the challenge of best leadership as helping others grow, to the extent that the leader does not even get any credit: "As for the best leaders, the people do not notice their existence. The next best, the people honour and praise. The next, the people fear; and the next, the people hate. When the best leader's work is done, his aim fulfilled, the people will say, 'We did it ourselves!'"

May you choose wisely the leader you want to be!

CHALLENGE 12

BELIEVE THAT THERE IS A BETTER WAY

A blind boy sat on the steps of a building with a hat by his feet. He held up a sign that said: "I am blind, please help."

There were only a few coins in the hat. A man was walking by. He took a few coins from his pocket and dropped them into the hat. He then took the sign, turned it around, and wrote several words. He put the sign back so that everyone who walked by would see the new words.

Soon, the hat began to fill up. A lot more people were giving money to the blind boy.

That afternoon, the man who had changed the sign came to see how things were. The boy recognised his footsteps and asked, "Were you the one who changed my sign this morning? What did you write?"

The man said, "I only wrote the truth. I said what you said but in a different way."

What he had written was: "Today is a beautiful day and I cannot see it."

Do you think the first sign and the second sign were saying the same thing? Of course both signs told people the boy was blind.

The first sign simply told people to help by putting some money in the hat. However, the second sign told people that they were able to enjoy the beauty of the day, but the boy could not enjoy it because he was blind.

The first sign simply said the boy was blind. The second sign told people they were so lucky that they were not blind. Should we be surprised that the second sign was more effective?

There are at least two lessons we can learn from this simple story.

The first is: Be thankful for what you have. Someone else has less. Help where you can.

The second is: Be creative. Be innovative. Think differently. There is always a better way!

As enunciated in Apple's 1997 *Think Different* commercial: "The people who are crazy enough to think they can change the world are the ones who do."